PRAISE
STUMBLING ON O

"Ken is jarringly honest about everything—life, success, fame, disillusionment, faith, questioning faith, cancer, the death of friends, and staying very close to one's spouse and Creator in the face of life-threatening challenges. This book might make you a little uncomfortable, but that's probably why you should read it. We must all at some point face similar challenges, face mortality, losing everything material, and Ken talks about what it's like to trust God, no matter what."

—BERNIE LEADON, FOUNDING MEMBER OF "THE EAGLES"

"Ken has been down roads so unique that many of us only read about lives like his in novels or see them in blockbuster movies. But this time, he gets personal and strikes a chord deep in our hearts as he tackles the universal questions of 'Why me? Why now? Will I be able to handle this? Where are you, God?' This book is sure to inspire you, and help you to doubt your doubts, and place your faith in God."

—KIRK CAMERON, ACTOR AND PRODUCER

"Ken Mansfield's *Stumbling on Open Ground* is one of the most extraordinary messages of healing—spiritual, physical and emotional—I have ever read. As someone who is paid to write, I'm genuinely in awe of his descriptive powers . . . and he needs them all to convey the Tolstoyan experiences of his past trials, and to describe the miraculous. Ken's writing is truly magnificent and this is a book that will be savored and remembered forever by those lucky enough to crack it open. Thank God for keeping Ken alive to write it."

—DAVID ASMAN, HOST OF *FORBES ON FOX*, FOX NEWS CHANNEL

"Ken Mansfield's harrowing journey from the pinnacle of success—on the rooftop with the Beatles for their final performance—to the depths of near death is a story both heavenly and hellish as he openly faces his God with the questions very few trust their heavenly Father enough to ask. God's answers lie between the pages of this book."

—MANCOW MULLER, NATIONALLY SYNDICATED
RADIO AND TELEVISION HOST

"From the first page you are immediately engaged and eager to see where each chapter will take you. When you read Ken's story you store up faith and courage for what may come your way no matter how great or small the trial. Plus, I love all the music bits! Ken has led a fascinating life that continues through his writings and zeal for whatever God puts before him. Read this book. You will be better for it."

—Rick Cua, pastoral care pastor, Grace Chapel, Leiper's Fork, Tennessee, and former bass player with the Outlaws

"You're going to love this book! Ken is creative, funny, and completely honest about life in a broken world—a world that includes cancer. You won't find plastic Christianity here. This is the real deal and it's terribly refreshing."

—Rev. Ivan Veldhuizen, pastor, executive director of International Ministries, Converge Worldwide

"Ken Mansfield is my favorite storyteller especially when he digs deep into the harder realities of life and faith. He always makes me think deeply—but he still makes me laugh out loud."

—Tommy Coomes, original member of legendary Love Song, former co-owner of Maranatha music

"What a life! What a walk! Ken Mansfield has been on the 'rooftop' of the world one moment and starting over as a low-level roadie humbly on his knees adjusting a stage monitor for a demanding diva the next. However, through the pages of *Stumbling on Open Ground*, we learn from Ken that when facing cancer everything about the past suddenly becomes unimportant. I've been privileged to know Ken. We have laughed and we have cried together. I love the Jesus that permeates him. His amazing journey fills me with such joy and hope . . . all because Ken loves Jesus and Jesus loves Ken."

—Brian Mason, legendary Christian radio personality

STUMBLING
on
OPEN GROUND

STUMBLING

on

OPEN GROUND

Love, God, Cancer, and
Rock 'n' Roll

KEN MANSFIELD

THOMAS NELSON
Since 1798

NASHVILLE   DALLAS   MEXICO CITY   RIO DE JANEIRO

Published in Nashville, Tennessee, by Thomas Nelson. Thomas Nelson is a registered trademark of Thomas Nelson, Inc.

Published in association with Rosenbaum & Associates Literary Agency, Nashville, Tennessee.

Thomas Nelson, Inc., titles may be purchased in bulk for educational, business, fundraising, or sales promotional use. For information, please e-mail SpecialMarkets@ ThomasNelson.com.

Unless otherwise noted, Scripture quotations are taken from The Living Bible (TLB) *The Living Bible.* © 1971. Used by permission of Tyndale House Publishers, Inc., Wheaton, Illinois 60189. All rights reserved.

Scriptures marked AMP are from THE AMPLIFIED BIBLE: OLD TESTAMENT. © 1962, 1964 by Zondervan (used by permission); and from THE AMPLIFIED BIBLE: NEW TESTAMENT. © 1958 by the Lockman Foundation (used by permission).

Library of Congress Cataloging-in-Publication Data

Mansfield, Ken.
  Stumbling on open ground : love, God, cancer, and rock'n' roll / Ken Mansfield.
    p. cm.
  Includes bibliographical references (p.   )
  ISBN 978-1-4002-0460-1
1. Mansfield, Ken. 2. Cancer--Patients--Religious life. 3. Christian biography--United States. 4. Sound recording executives and producers--United States--Biography. I. Title.
  BV4910.33.M335 2012
  248.8'61969940092--dc23
  [B]

                              2012028580

Printed in the United States of America

12 13 14 15 QG 6 5 4 3 2 1

CONTENTS

CONTENTS

If racing with mere men . . . has wearied you,
how will you race against horses . . .
If you stumble and fall on open ground,
what will you do in Jordan's jungles?

—JEREMIAH 12:5

TOMORROW NEVER KNOWS

There was something incredibly eerie about looking down on the ground and seeing John's face staring up at me. His eyes, as always, peering out with that questioning look—those eyes that followed you everywhere—not just physically, but once you looked into them, eyes that grabbed on to you with unsaid words that screamed into your soul. I was kneeling as he stared up at me, trying to get a sense of what had happened. In the stillness, I felt as if we were asking the same questions. I could feel them unite as they dissolved into the haze that surrounded this moment. He had been shot, and the many days of his life had just drained out onto a dark New York sidewalk.

It had just happened, a few long minutes ago, but I wasn't there at the Dakota on the cold cement with him. I was on my knees on the floor of my office in Hollywood, far away on the other side of the continent, sorting through pictures to put on the walls of my new music production company. The irony of spreading out pictures from the Apple Records days across my office floor a matter of minutes before I answered the phone call that told me of John's demise landed me in a daze. I was surprised at my reaction. There he was staring up at me from a picture he had sent me a few years before when I was running the Beatles' record company in America. The words written across the bottom: "I am at 3 Savile Row, most days."

I was confused, wedged between the joy of great memories of that exciting time working with him and his bandmates, and now, the profound sadness of this event that suddenly invaded my life. I moved back into the fabric of universal bereavement and relinquished any sense of privilege or personal loss. I ceased seeing John Lennon as someone I had known and worked with, but instead found myself staring into the face of our inescapable mortality. *We're so young. Where did this come from? This is not what we do.*

This shattering moment was our generation's 9/11. Nothing would ever be the same in the world where celebrities once freely moved around at will. A bewildered fan crossed a line that had never been crossed before in our time, and all of a sudden, the No Trespassing sign into our privileged status had been permanently torn down. We were used to being intruded upon while eating a simple meal in a fancy restaurant, which was an accepted price for fame. But—this? The stars were now afraid to come out at night.

I looked up from my folded stance on the floor. My eyes examined the walls and shelves of my office, surveying the trophies of a hedonistic world—gold-plated things that reflected the rewards of a glamorous life. I wondered what it all meant. What if I, too, was suddenly removed from existence? I was not a

Christian then, but I began mulling over such matters—matters of eternity. These trinkets would be left alone here without me and I would be somewhere alone without them. Everything seemed so pointless. Having only my narrow perspective to draw upon left me completely disoriented—so baffled that I stopped thinking about it. My personal reckoning was just a flash. I now wish I had reflected on the wisdom before me a little longer. What *would* happen to me when I left my stuff behind?

I fell forward onto the floor, crumpling the pictures in my hands. I began to cry, not sure where the tears were coming from. I didn't even cry when my dad died. I can't remember anything that happened the rest of that afternoon.

In the following days we gathered together over the phone and in person, in our tight little geographical unit—Ringo Starr, Harry Nilsson, Delaney and Bonnie's manager Alan Pariser, and me, the ragged remains of the LA posse of musical marauders. We went to a private screening of Harry's new movie *Popeye* as soon as Ringo returned from paying his respects to Yoko in New York. A night out on the town with old friends was Ringo's idea and a way to get away from it all. Afterward, sequestered in a private dining room of a Beverly Hills restaurant, nobody talked about it. The subject stayed off topic for years.

Shots from a cold gun became the startling wake-up call to our era and there was no snooze button to give us a little more time. The message was that it was time for us, the survivors, to understand that we had to deal with the odds like everyone else, even admitting that our rarified air had the same germs in it that everyone breathes.

The phone rings and I am jolted out of that reflective mood, out of an era when we thought we were so invincible, and back into current reality. It's another mortality call—not John's but mine. This call comes years later and I am looking at that same picture on a different wall of a different office and at a different time. The roles are now reversed. His picture hangs there above me and he is looking down on me as I get news about a different sort of bullet. This time it's aimed at me.

I look up into those eyes. The questions and the unknowing still remain. John Lennon never saw it coming. Neither did I. Tomorrow really never knows, does it? Only God has that figured out.

DEEP IN THE JUNGLE

was once told that walking is merely controlled falling—the organization, discipline, and catching of our forward momentum. My Christian walk looks like that at times, like controlled stumbling. I am on open ground because I am a believer, and yet I am in constant search of an end to the aggravating and seemingly perpetual tottering of my spiritual walk. I am fully aware that God has made the way smooth, and I have his promise that if I stray, he will gently put me back on the path. All I have to do is believe and seek him with all my heart.

I also believe that God is God Almighty and that he is perfect and makes no mistakes. I believe the Holy Bible is the inspired Word of God and that every word in the Word is true. I am totally there, head, hands, heart, and what little hair I have left. But, like many Christians, there are certain questions I can't answer. I have trouble sometimes understanding how it all works on a mechanical level.

I find myself puzzled and pondering over things that creep into my mind and heart, causing confusion in the core of my beliefs—the kinds of things that make us lose our balance as we try to imagine what it will be like someday to walk about the halls of heaven while we're still down here shuffling around in our man-made flip-flops. I want to walk in his footsteps. I am not going anywhere else—I've already been there. For me there is no turning back. I squandered my inheritance and wallowed in the decadence of both the high life and low life. I have eaten the food meant for pigs. Now I wear the warm robe of forgiveness because Jesus ran to me from a distance and welcomed me home. I drink from the well of living water and am fed to fullness by the Bread of Life. The taste in my mouth is sweet from the ever-flowing nectar of new wine. My golden cup runneth over, and just to be seated at the foot of his table is the supreme joy in my life.

But I don't always like the soup of the day at this table. What do I do when I am served up a rare, incurable cancer? What do I do when, in the process of living and trusting him through this trial, I am given another portion—and this time it is a mean, burning second dose of the disease?

The first one was slow and even though it responded to treatment, it's incurable, a treacherous partner to the end. I am told it could stay "indolent" and just sit there with minimal aggravation—or it can decide to make its move at any time, a ticking-time-bomb situation where only God knows the length of the fuse. While the first cancer had been calmed down by chemical therapy, the second cancer came raging in, blindsiding and brutal, here and now, all or nothing, no time for contemplating or experimenting. Regardless of my personal resistance to heavy chemotherapy and heavier radiation, the choice was literally do-or-die. It was a coin toss; the treatment could do me in, and so could the cancer. But I had a chance to live, and I realized there were no other choices. I bowed my head to the reality of my situation and bowed my heart to the reality of God's lordship and love. Somehow it made sense. I just didn't know how at that time.

The minute I received the news that I would be facing a second battle, I turned to God for direction. I announced to him and myself, both out loud and from my heart, that I would never doubt him through this trial. He knows my heart, and I know his. Understanding is not a part of the deal; obedience is what he asks.

This is a quest for deeper comprehension, a desire to dip beneath the opaque surface. As a child, I would ask my earthly father how to do things. As a child of God, I am asking my heavenly Father how this all works between him and me.

I never question him. But I do wonder at times about myself.

Book One

BODEGA BAY, CALIFORNIA

1996–2002

Chapter 1
THE BEGINNING OF THE EDGE

December 1996, Santa Rosa, California

He appeared calm as he scanned the results. "I have gone over your recent blood work, and I want to have a special lab run some additional tests." The look on his face was relaxed and matter-of-fact. I could tell it was nothing serious. He was just being thorough—he was a "specialist" in his field, after all.

The atmosphere and mood in the warmly appointed office was very laid-back that day. It was my first time visiting his practice, and though I did not know this doctor, I was comfortable there. I had been sent to see him by my family doctor because of his specialty, rheumatology. The medical form he held in his hand had to do with the results of the blood tests he requested for arthritis in my knees. In going over the paperwork, he noticed a small spike in one of the tests that had nothing to do with his area of expertise. The odd little indicator required an explanation, so one specialist was sending me to another.

He handed me a piece of paper with an address and a little map on the back showing how to get there. I never worry about those kinds of tests, in part because of an old friend and mentor at Capitol Records many years ago who displayed a plaque behind his desk with a quote from sixteenth-century essayist and statesman, Michel de Montaigne:

MY LIFE HAS BEEN FILLED WITH MANY MISFORTUNES,
MOST OF WHICH HAVE NEVER HAPPENED.

I have forgotten many of the things this great man said, but the words on his office wall stayed with me. Driving away from the doctor's office I knew it was all good—nothing to worry about.

Connie and I lived in Bodega Bay at the time, and the address on the small slip of paper was in Santa Rosa, California, about forty-five minutes from our home by the ocean.

The appointment was scheduled for eleven thirty in the morning the following week. Because that location was on the north end of town, we decided that after the consultation and lab work we would head into the adjacent wine country, have a nice lunch, and maybe do some wine tasting in Healdsburg. We loved the little town square there, and the drive back through the vineyards and coastal ranges is very scenic. If we timed it just right, we would be driving home into the filtered sunset. The days were short, but the weather was nice that time of year. We would take the day off and have some fun.

The day of the appointment came, and things were already off to a bad start. At that time Connie was an associate director in television (*Hee Haw*, the Dove Awards) and currently working on *The Statler Brothers Show* on cable TV. Early that morning I put her on a plane in San Francisco and drove back north to Santa Rosa for my afternoon appointment. This was supposed to be a fun day in Sonoma County, but my appointment kept getting pushed back until it collided with Connie's career. Nashville called; the taping schedule was tight, and it would keep her for at least a week.

I went alone.

Following the directions on my slip of paper, I rounded the last corner on my way to my destination and was shocked when I saw the street number I was looking for etched on a sign that read, Oncology Center. What was I doing here?

Things went into slow motion. What did this have to do with itchy knee sockets? Maybe it simply had to do with the equipment, or maybe this was the only place that housed a particular medical feature in our area.

I parked a long way from the entrance, a sort of logistical denial of the sign on the street, and entered a world I had never seen before. I couldn't help looking away in the lobby waiting room as I saw pale and emaciated young people, many without hair, moving listlessly about the area among old women and older men with gaunt eyes and lifeless faces. Bandannas on women. Crutches leaning against the side of a chair where a sad old man sat. Bags with pumps and tubes going into different noses and up various sleeves. It was all so alien and distant. Scary.

When I got on the elevator to the second floor where I was instructed to go, I felt such pity for these people who had *cancer*. *Oh, my God, how sad. Cancer!*

I waited almost an hour in a waiting room with dull beige walls and those horrible plant sketches, meticulously laid out in rows, subscripted with their Latin names. The reading choices on the worn, mismatched end tables were slim: *Fish and Game* and *Women's Wear Daily*. Overhead, Muzak played while I waited—cheesy arrangements of songs like "Light My Fire" and "Good Vibrations." Talk about melodious oxymoronics. It did allow me to relive some of the excitement of my thirty years in the music business. I smiled—and winced a bit—to think that someone had the nerve to do *that* to such classic songs. After what felt like an eternity and four bars into a horn-heavy, full-orchestral version of "Stairway to Heaven," I really began to feel agitated. As a one-time record producer, I can just picture the looks on the faces of the bored musicians as they played on these recordings. It was funny for a while, but about thirty minutes into the evaporated milk arrangements I wanted to bolt. I felt alone, but was able to push off that feeling by reading about how to drill a proper hole for ice fishing in the barren reaches of Alaska.

Then the nurse finally showed up and ushered me into an even blander examination room with more fine art on the wall. The pink-and-red gallbladders had more detail and were much more colorful than the sepia-brown and faded-green stems and leaves in the waiting room. I read the words on the gutsy poster over and over. I was really trying to keep it together, but they were not even coming close to meeting me halfway. What should play next from the overhead speaker in the corner of the ceiling but a salsa rendition of "Feelings." Perfect. At this point, I was clinging to the edge.

But no deliverance just yet. I was given the privilege of spending another forty-five minutes under the exceptionally bright neon overheads. Having read the names of various organs and their interesting blood supplies about ten times, I finally stood up and was reading the small labels on the tape dispensers when the new specialist—call him Dr. Doornail—walked in.

I wondered how he kept from bumping into things, because

all I could see was the top of his bald head. He kept his face buried in my medical chart in what was obviously a first-time read. I love it when someone gives you the cold-fish handshake without looking up at you—especially with that schmaltzy version of "Feelings" still bouncing around in my head.

I did not belong here. I did not like this little man. I did not like the way he looked, the way he checked me over. It was very clinical and by rote. We were ten minutes into the examination, and I still didn't know the color of his eyes. More than all that, I especially did not like what he had to say. "We have a preliminary diagnosis of multiple myeloma. Have you ever heard of it? It's a cancer of the plasma cells in your bone marrow and . . . blah . . . blah . . . blah . . . blah . . . blah . . ."

Either I drifted off or finally fell off the edge from the cold technical drone of his explanation. Trombones filled the air. If Paul McCartney had known that a brassy version of "Yesterday" would fill the tinny speakers of these halls, I think he would have rather died before writing a note. Even more horrifying, I imagined the nightmare scenario of Sir Paul being tied down while they played this rendition nonstop until he cracked! Too terrible to contemplate. Then, as twin accordions filled the air in place of violin accompaniment, I was jolted back to the immediate conversation.

"Before we make a final diagnosis, I do want to do another test while you are here. We should have a final fix on this little feller in about a week. Take off your clothes and put on this gown." Things were moving a little fast and off-course for me at this point, especially hearing I had something that didn't sound good from Dr. Doornail, who called it a "little feller." Of course being able to put on one of the hospital's designer, open-air, rear-view gowns did soften things a bit. Donovan's "Catch the Wind" played from the ceiling—nice clarinet ensemble.

What happened next was unexpected, unwanted, and unbelievably brutal. A robotic team with metal trays walked in and instructed me to lie down on my side on the exam table. (Whatever happened to hello?) They proceeded to take a bone marrow sample. Nothing to it, just another test! Just lookin' for that "little feller" by going through my left buttock to the center of my hip bone with a needle the diameter of a garden hose. The needle had a hole big enough to insert a pair of tiny tweezers that grabbed a bit of marrow from the center of the bone. I have a rule of only crying about sad songs or during baptisms, but this really hurt.

The medical technician performing the biopsy told me that some people have no problem with the procedure—"they don't even feel it." Maybe. But if you have a pulse, it's excruciating. *This is not the start of something good,* I thought to myself. They moved about nonchalantly after the procedure and walked away leaving me stunned and feeling bushwhacked. (Whatever happened to goodbye?) I was flabbergasted—and in pain.

When the nurse came in to put a small bandage over the tiny hole in my skin, she noticed that I was lying there with my eyes wide open as if I had just grabbed hold of an electric fence. She asked how it went. When I told her how I felt, she remarked that I must be one of those creative types. "You people do respond a little more delicately than normal people." She sighed and left the room. I lay there alone for what seemed an eternity.

Are we done or are there more tests? No tellin' where else that "little feller" could be lurking in my body. It's a little bit lonely here, even though my southern exposure is enjoying the breeze.

I looked over, and the gallbladders began to dance with the

transverse colon on the wall. That's when I knew it was time to get out of there. I got dressed and practically ran down the hall with my untied shoelaces smacking the marble floor. The repetitive digital glitch on "(I Can't Get No) Satisfaction" back in the hell room was the last straw.

I ran through the lobby without looking at anyone or anything, stumbled to my car, got in, started it up, and pulled out of the parking lot in a complete daze. I turned right on the road that brought me there and drifted to the stoplight at the bottom of the hill. It was a long light. With my hands on the steering wheel at ten and two, I dropped my forehead to the wheel and froze. I couldn't move, even with the horns honking behind me and distant voices suggesting I simultaneously get the car and my battered tail in gear and move on.

I eventually regrouped, took the back roads to Bodega Bay, and drove out to Doran Beach on the southern end of the bay, just as the sun was beginning to set. I parked the car at the edge of the dunes, took off my shoes, and walked to the water's edge. Those were edges I could understand. I like the fact that it is always different there. I looked down at my watch to calculate Nashville time. I needed to call Connie.

I turned to leave but stopped, turned back around, and stood facing the fading day across the water. It had been warm inland. I had no jacket, so I pulled myself around me. I closed my eyes and prayed. I felt God's peace wash over me.

I opened my eyes and stared at the edge of the horizon. I wished I could see farther, but it was okay.

I needed to call Connie.

Chapter 2
CANCERS AND CADILLACS

I try to remember what life was like before cancer invaded our lives in December 1996. At least that's when it reared its ugly head; it had been lurking a few years prior to diagnosis. It's that unwelcome houseguest I read about somewhere. It's a dark cloud that hangs overhead and never leaves. It's always in the back of my mind and tearing at my heart and soul. I try to put my trust in God, but I guess I don't, not really, because I'm still scared, and fear is not of him.

Ken has always been so strong in the midst of adversity (which is where I met him, so I really don't know him any other way). There have been a few reprieves over the years—sweet, brief moments. It's our way of life to live by the edge, that's the way Ken loves to live, even physically—like where we lived then, right at the edge of the ocean. It seems the trials he is given are always huge! The cancer diagnosis was no exception.

I can remember attending our little Fisherman's Chapel in Bodega Bay a couple of years before Ken's diagnosis. I was always asking for prayer and that "we find out what's wrong with my husband!" He had been misdiagnosed and in pain for so long.

Our faithful pastor, Art Wright, a gentle man, full of great compassion for the entire human race and all creatures great and small, prayed fervently for the answers. We finally got them. Sometimes I wish we hadn't.

—Connie

turned from the darkened waters and my time with God. I crossed the dunes and I was surprised to hear the idling motor of my waiting car. Not only had I left the motor running, I had also left the door open and the radio on, which was then blaring away—Jimi Hendrix's "Purple Haze."

A young couple, parked a few yards away in a shiny Cadillac convertible with the top down, stared at me as if I were daft. I acted as if I meant for the door to be ajar, the music blasting and the motor running. With flair and calm authority I drug myself and a pound of damp sand on my feet into the open driver's side, turned the music up even louder, revved the motor a couple of times, burned a short patch of rubber as I backed up, and headed up the hill toward home.

The house was cold and dark when I arrived. It was dinnertime, but I was not hungry. Time felt as if it had stopped, but I knew I needed to keep moving.

I lit one of those "fake," easy-burning logs in our fireplace and began wrapping Christmas presents, diving deep in thought as I wrapped my defenses around me in reluctant preparation of what was to come. When I finally ran out of things to keep my head, hands, and heart busy, I stood up. But once I was standing, I couldn't move. My head dropped to my chest, my arms fell to my side, and I became lost in the silence. I needed to call Connie.

I needed Connie.

I went to the refrigerator and checked the TV taping schedule she had placed there; it was a good time to call. I dialed the phone; it only rang once. She had been waiting.

When I heard that rich, soft voice, I was immediately comforted. Connie's voice was one of the things that knocked me out the first time I called her for a date. She listened quietly as I told her about the cancer diagnosis and the day's events. I could picture her alone in her hotel room: eyes closed, head bowed down. There were really no words to be exchanged, just tears and a deep understanding of how much we meant to each other. We held the phones in silence almost as if we were holding on to each other.

I hung up the phone and looked out the window into a silent dusk. We had taken longer than I thought, and the room I was standing in once again became real. It had lost its warmth, and I felt chilly. I wrapped one of her shawls around my shoulders—it smelled like her so I didn't feel so lonely. I pulled my favorite chair up to a window that looked out at the bay and watched the whitecaps roll in and out against the shore. There was just enough moonlight to highlight the edges of the waves. I settled there with my feet placed up on the windowsill, and then I fell apart in the secluded silence.

I began praying so hard for healing that Bill O'Reilly would have had a hard time getting a word in edgewise. These pleadings eventually evolved into one of my one-sided conversations with God. I had to talk to him about what was going on so he could understand my situation more clearly. I began running out my standard list of needs, counting on him to be a good listener. I rattled on for a while covering topics like unfairness, why he was doing this to me, and my usual list of worldly stuff. Then he suddenly interrupted me.

It was like someone turned off my mic. Did I die, or just run out of words? Either way, everything became calm. I experienced one of those rare moments when I stopped my ramblings and heard a sweet, soft voice that swept over my soul like a warm wind. There were no words or sounds—just impartations into that place inside that knows certain things. When this happened, everything came to a complete stop, and the only thing left stirring was my heart and his majesty.

In the special way he speaks to me, God reminded me that he is a healing God. *Now, that's what I wanted to hear.* I finally began to relax. Knowing that there was going to be healing around the corner was enough to make the trial and pain easier to handle. He continued, and here's the tricky part—it came to me that I wouldn't know whether he was going to heal me during my lifetime or wait until I joined him in eternity, where I would be completely healed. So I stayed relaxed. I knew I was going to be healed, eventually.

This may seem a little abstract, but I understood what he was saying, and it really worked for me. Heal me now, and he would be glorified as the result of the earthly outcome; or heal me later when it would be perfect healing. Either way was okay; either way was reassuring. It was all in his perfect plan, somehow. I made the decision a long time ago that I had to make a choice—either I believe or I don't. And down in my guts I knew he would see me through. Cancer or any other malady is not a forever thing. But eternity *is* a forever thing, and that is where those of us who believe in him dwell. Deadly cancers and worldly Cadillacs are nothing but fleeting glimpses of the world we live in.

Eternity. Now that's the real long part of our existence.

17

Chapter 3
DYING AND DOING

When this all began happening, I was commuting back and forth from Bodega Bay to Nashville to do television projects where I worked as an associate director. Sometimes I would be gone for a month at a time. I was in a Nashville hotel room when Ken called to tell me that he had been sent to see an oncologist in Santa Rosa and he was told that he had cancer. I felt so helpless and frightened to be so far away from my husband during these crucial times when we really needed to be together, to cling to each other for comfort. I'm sure God knew that we needed to go through some of this alone. His ideas aren't always ours. I can't even express how hard that truly was.

—Connie

was called back to the clinic ten days later for a consultation with Dr. Doornail. After a long wait, he rushed in with his clipboard in hand and an assistant trailing behind with a stack of paper. The results from the bone marrow sample and other blood work were in, and the news was even worse than expected—it wasn't multiple myeloma after all (another misdiagnosis). I was told that the new test results were definitive, and that I had an extremely rare and incurable cancer of the lymphatic system instead.

Doornail neither paused nor looked up to see if this information had any effect on me or how I may have felt about the news. How about that? Just days before Christmas, and I was being told that I have a cancer that cuts my life expectancy down to three, maybe five years. I was also informed that besides being incurable, there was also very little research being done on this particular form of cancer due to its rarity. As I had been ill and misdiagnosed the two years preceding this new discovery, the doctors felt I had used up two of my too-few years. Surprise! I was looking at one to three years of a dwindling existence. My mind automatically latched on to the single, solitary, one-year bit, which made the whole situation even more dramatic.

He then launched into an explanation that sounded as if he was dictating notes into a machine. His discourse was technically over my head, but I think if you have either worked on a used-car lot or been in the music business for a few years, you develop an unusually keen sense of when someone is presenting something to you that doesn't add up.

It was obvious to me that an element of professional jive was coming down. Bottom line: he was telling me that with this particular diagnosis, the facility would qualify for a lucrative research grant if they had a sufficient number of candidates that fit specific criteria for a new chemotherapy study program. Mine was one of the "incurables" that was in that group. I was exactly what they were looking for. Lucky me. I wasn't able to spell, pronounce, or even mouth the names of the drugs or procedures that were listed on the pages in that stack of papers, but deep down I knew I didn't want any of that stuff put in me. I felt a lot of pressure from their presentation, and naturally they wanted to start immediately.

Now it was my turn to be inconsiderate. I didn't respond. I didn't accept the signing pen and paper being handed to me. I turned. I left. I was becoming very good at running out of that building.

When I left the oncology center that time, things were different. I got tough inside. I can't explain the feeling. It wasn't as though I had scriptures flowing in and out of my head, that I was mad at God, that I was resting in his promises, or that I became resigned to anything. Instead, I became a blank canvas waiting for a clear picture to be painted inside me. I wasn't lost, found, or in between anything. I felt a strength I had never felt before and knew that I didn't need to define it.

I had Pink Floyd's "Momentary Lapse of Reason" cranked way up on my car stereo as I headed for Bodega Bay. As I got closer to the ocean, pieces came together in my head. It was as if there were an exchange going on inside, and the only reason I was included was because it was taking place in my head and was about my body. There is an incredible difference between knowing you are going to die someday and actually going about the business of doing it. You don't get a lot of practice. When it does eventually become your turn to give it a go, you might discover a certain unyieldingness of spirit that is curiously juxtaposed with a bewildering sense of acceptance as the whole unwieldy process unfolds. A complicated dichotomy sets in, and its machinations become the norm as you bounce back and forth between reality, notions, imagination, and imbedded misconceptions about how things are supposed to be.

I drove straight home. I didn't want to look at the ocean. I didn't want its comfort, its lapping, enveloping rhythms.

The house was cold, and I didn't want to be warm.

I stopped in the middle of the room and closed my eyes. I did everything I could to empty out my mind, my heart, and conceptions about my place in the world. I only wanted to go numb. I finally opened my eyes, and the room came back into focus. I realized that I'd been standing alone in nothing but darkness for more than an hour. I also realized that the empty place inside was being filled up with something good.

I headed for the bedroom, and with every step, I felt a Presence joining me as I walked down the hall. I undressed amid the strange calm, and before I lay down, I wrote the following in my journal:

Today I found out I have incurable cancer. It is a few days before Christmas, and my reaction is one of peace. I am disappointed to hear this news, but at the same time I have an uncanny sense of relief. Being a Christian really comes in handy in times like these. It is almost like God is beginning to reveal a new stage in my life. Deep within, where his comforting Holy Spirit dwells, I feel clarity in the mysterious—understanding of the unknown—vision into the unseen. I am in his purpose and that is all I need to know.

I woke up early the next morning and was stunned by how I felt—a strange euphoria. I had a deep sense of peace and was filled with a sweet, simple joy. This sense of serenity and well-being seemed out of place given my devastating diagnosis the day before. It was then that I felt as if God walked up to me, put his arm around my shoulders, and told me we were going to go through an incredible experience together. Once again, there were no words—just wisdom and truth and comfort flooding my being. He let me know that the incredible peace I was experiencing was his gift to me, something available to everyone.

God told me that the way I felt meant that I truly believed in him and trusted him. I could rest in the comfort that my faith was real. What I was feeling was the peace that truly does pass all understanding—a peace you can't understand until you have it. Because God knew this was a big deal to me, he let me know he was in it with me—big time—and the way it would play out would amaze me. He also reminded me that he is God and doesn't always let us know what he has in mind.

He described two possible outcomes. If he decided to take me home via my illness, then I would be in heaven with him. That was actually very good news. I already knew heaven was where I wanted to be more than anything, so that was cool. If he decided to heal me, then I could spend my time in glorifying him and his miraculous healing ways. I could be used as a witness to his mercy and grace; and in time, through this process, even more people would end up sharing heaven with me.

I grabbed my Bible, broke it open to some of its most worn places, and began searching favorite scriptures. I needed God's help in understanding and accepting the fact that a lethal disease had entered my life and that it was as simple as he just described. I admit that I was bouncing about a bit as I tried to fit an untidy circumstance into my familiar and neat little world.

I pulled myself deeper into my Bible until I found myself inserted into the words. The unknown road before me, the book in front of me, and the thoughts of my past adventures all came together and created a strange and inspiring sort of momentum. If I was of the earth, then I had all these earthen things in me; and my journey across the spiritual landscape told me I was a bit of everything. If I were part of a sentence, I would be a transitional phrase. I was trying to move from sinful thoughts and bad ideas to the mind of Christ, one that thinks the thoughts of God, a mind that accepts his plans for me as if they were my own idea. No wonder I was struggling.

I realized something. It is not unnatural that I would have these worldly and heavenly thoughts at the same time. I am a man of the soil, a man with a soul, who had the divine life of God and the mind of Christ planted in me when I accepted Jesus as my Savior. I am all these things, all at once.

As Jesus taught when he also became a man of the soil and walked among soiled men, I must learn to deal with things in their proper order and priority, even precious things like my life, my fears about dying, and my fears for Connie. At that moment I thought, *When my priorities match his, that is how I'll know I am finally becoming more like him.*

What an incredible journey.

If I get it right, I please him.

If I get it wrong, he loves me and gives me another chance.

Because of him I am filled with joy knowing that I am blessed among men.

Chapter 4

CREDIT CARD STATEMENT

At first, Ken was misdiagnosed with multiple myeloma, which was scary enough. It wasn't long after the bone-marrow biopsy that they finally were able to make the correct diagnosis. The cancer has a hard name to learn: Waldenström's macroglobu-linemia (WM). It's a malignant and rare type of slow-growing non-Hodgkin lymphoma that begins in the cells of the immune system. It causes overproduction of a protein antibody called IgM [monoclonal immunoglobulin M]; it's considered an "orphan disease" because so few people are diagnosed with it. Approximately fifteen hundred cases are diagnosed each year in the United States, and it is not yet curable.[1] The prognosis back then was three to five years of life, and the doctors believed he had it at least a couple of years prior because of the history of his symptoms. We were on rabbit trail for at least that long before finding out.

—Connie

T his was a learning experience. We were not ready for any of it. Who is? And because of our lack of experience, Connie and I were at a loss in how to discuss it, understand it, or even figure out how to go about it.

Before I knew the Lord, I always took care of my calamities by myself. Since I became a believer, married Connie, and we became one, we have always been able to team up to face and conquer challenges together with God's help. Up until that point, though, I had always had a hand in the problem solving and bringing about some form of a solution. But I admit, this was beyond me, and it even felt beyond the oneness of our marriage.

Was it beyond my faith too?

I picked up my Bible, and it fell open to Psalm 33:4–7, where I have one of dozens of emergency-moment bookmarkers. (I have tried opening my Bible at random when I need answers, but I always land on a page with no underlining—one that's usually filled with instructions on how to sacrifice animals or measure tabernacles. Instead of doing this, I put odd pieces of paper, business cards, or plastic inserts between the pages as bookmarks to key verses that have spoken to me over the years.) The page before me had an old credit-card statement sticking out, and the message there confronted me and comforted me:

F OR ALL GOD'S WORDS ARE RIGHT, AND EVERYTHING he does is worthy of our trust. He loves whatever is just and good; the earth is filled with his tender love. He merely spoke, and the heavens were formed, and all the galaxies of stars. He made the oceans, pouring them into his vast reservoirs.

I was banking on it.

I was alone. It was dusk, and I looked out the window and saw the vast expanse of the Bodega Bay harbor and shore. I looked down and saw that I had been squeezing my Bible so hard it had leapt out of my hand. It had finished with me. It just gave me my directions. I needed to go to the edge and let it go. I needed my Father to take care of this one. Even though Connie was in Nashville on a TV location surrounded by people, I knew she, too, would find somewhere to pray alone.

I walked down the hill to the beach, stopped where the sand and waters met, and began praying out toward the horizon.

FATHER, I LOVE THE SEARCH—THE INVOLVEMENT of trying to place my will into yours. I wish I could reach out to you all the time like I do when I am really hurting and pleading on my knees for your presence within me. In the fleeting moments when everything seems okay, I miss the searing intensity of your all-consuming fire blazing in my face—when conviction is hot on my trail and the heat of the trial burns your purpose into my heart. Like a moth, I want to dive into the flame of your truth, die to myself, and then come alive in the pure light of your everlasting love. I long for that special feeling I get when I lay it all down and recognize you as my source, my provider, my everything. My greatest moments are when I feel something touching that spot I just can't put my finger on—that place where you have your hand on me. It's the place from which I reach out to you when I start spinning out, sinking out of sight, plummeting out of control and uncovered into the mire of my selfishness, my will, and my way.

Oh Father, wherever you are, reach down and hear my cry. Sometimes I look out across this bay and everything diffuses into prismatic splendor as the tears of worship cloud my eyes and run down my face, beneath my collar and into my soul. Prayers, scriptures, pleadings, and confusion swirl and whirl around me like a tempest across the waves. I become lost in you. I am suspended where there is no space and time, where there is only the awesome unknown that is you before me.

My eyes focused on an odd spot on the sea just short of the horizon, a bit off to the left and a glimpse away from the edge of the sky—a place I had never looked at before. In meditation, I sank down into the deep blue of the lonely sea at that place and became immersed in his Word as his promises flowed over me. Peace prevailed, and he joined me in the depths and comforted me with his perfection and unconditional love.

Then the sea parted and, like Jonah, I was tossed out on dry land. *He saves me; I am saved; he is my Savior,* I thought. *He provides the fiery light that leads me, the manna that feeds me, and I no longer murmur ingratitude. If only I could realize that the cloud on the horizon before me is an Old Testament cloud of protection and guidance—if only I could stop questioning him and just follow his all-consuming fire to the promised land.*

I prayed:

O H FATHER, WHEREVER YOU ARE, I LONG FOR THAT same place. Like Jacob, I wish you would wrestle me to the ground, change my name to Faithful and True, and change my walk. Give me a noticeable limp and a clear path. Oh Father, wherever you are, let me come to you and sit under the shelter of your grace as your glory blinds me to my desires. Please teach me about the cross, about what really happened that day. Help me to understand your magnificence and the perfect blend of tragedy and victory that took place on that barren, windswept hill. Startle me with the immensity of that moment when "it was finished" and I became gloriously blessed with eternal salvation. I am tired of running ragged around the edges of the torn curtain. Pull me further, Father—farther up the hill of my destiny—and set me before the triple trees of Golgotha. Let me fall within the gaze of the man in the middle. Because I believe in him so deeply, let me hear the sweet sound of his voice, of his forgiveness and the astounding invitation to join him in eternity.

Suddenly the warm waves of his mercy embraced me on the shore of that quiet seaside village. I picked myself up and made my way up the beach toward home.

Was I limping or was that just my imagination?

Chapter 5
MISSING IN ATTITUDE

Ken decided he wanted to keep this news quiet and only share with our closest friends and family, for their love and support, and especially their prayers. It was hard for me to pretend that all was well, but I did a pretty good job of it. Nevertheless, I was able to share and pray with my closest friends, and that was very comforting.

I never really understood why he wanted to keep it quiet until the word finally got out. That's when I got it. It was as if the cancer became Ken's identity, with folks always asking, "How are you, really?"

—Connie

onnie has always been so open and honest about everything. She was uncomfortable with concealing reality, and I was lousy at facing situations so completely out of my control. I had never had my faith tested like that before; my walk with the Lord had actually been very easy up to this point. But this situation made me feel like a deer in the headlights. I had everything I needed in order to keep from being run over, but I darted about—confused about what I knew about him and what he knows about me.

I am probably like many Christians in that I spend a lot of my time trying to figure out which way to go, but then when I remember he is God, it takes only a moment to stop and rest in him and his promises. Even though I know his mercies are new every morning, why is it that every morning I stumble on open promises? *I stumble new every morning, new every morning, oh great is my stumbling, oh Lord . . . great is my stumbling!*

It was early in the game, and I was having one of those lost-in-the-glare days where as far as I could tell God was missing. I looked for him everywhere, and he was missing! I walked and searched by the water's edge. I became still before the sea; I waited—I listened and heard nothing. I cried out and there was no answer. I covered myself by praying his exact words from the Psalms—I knew he could not deny me then. He must respond, right? He must answer. He must speak. He must solve, repair, enhance, enable, lift, protect, give, save, and modify my situation. Why else would I have a God? Wasn't he here for me and my doing? I set the stage and he does the act, right?

Can I say I am like Peter, Paul, Job, or even Esther without sounding pompous? I read of their deeds, trials, and purposes and find myself lost in their love and their frustrations. In one chapter, Peter went from the man Christ found so faithful and righteous that he called him the rock,[1] to the man he called Satan and rebuked—"Get away from me, you Satan!" a few verses later.[2] I realize that Jesus loved Peter at both edges: saint and sinner, religious and sacrilegious, rock and brimstone edges. I realize I also fit at different times in this spectrum of obedience and faithlessness. I change and vacillate, but Jesus is always the same. He loves me, hangs in there with me, even hung on a cross for me. He was hanging in there with me then as I bounced around the walls of my own upper room.

I am like Paul in that I try to do what is right. I want to be obedient and pure, and yet I have these thoughts; I behave in ways that are outside God's purpose, outside his ways, outside his pleasure. I want to be pleasing to him. I want to be good and godly, but then, like a fool I do the very things that he and I both do not want me to do. I go bonkers with my stupidity and he keeps on loving me. What is wrong with this picture? Maybe I should ask myself, *What is right with this picture?*

I struggle outwardly with my actions while he waits for me to settle down and bring my struggle to him. I labor inside my reactions and he is the calm before, after, and during the storm—always available, always ready to comfort, guide, and hold me close. I wish I could love him like he loves me.

Who is missing?

I go over the edge physically, spiritually, and geographically while he stands in place—arms outstretched, promises intact and always available. He is perpetually moving toward me by remaining fixed in his love for me. I often pray for great spiritual memory so I can remember his directions when trials appear, then he answers my prayer, and I reject the Word and accept turmoil instead. He offers the peace that passes all understanding, and then in my earthly nature I pass on his peace and can't understand why my wheels keep falling off. He will guide me; he will grant me wisdom; he will protect me and provide for me in every situation. I know that.

So, from the water's edge, I came before the Lord, Creator of all time, the Teacher of all things, the Master of eternal matters, and the Servant of all. I asked him to forgive me, to hold me in his everlasting, precious arms, comfort me, speak to me, guide me, grant me the simple gift of surrender so I could be pleasing unto his purpose in my life. I came to him; I bowed before him; I worshipped him; and I pled with him:

L ORD, YOU ASKED THE LEPER IN YOUR WORD, "WHAT do you want?" I beseech you to heal me—if you want to. Say to me as you said to him, "of course I want to," and then let me be healed immediately of this cancer. Let me be healed so I can be sent out to speak of your almighty power, grace, mercy, and love.

I love you, I praise you, I adore you, and I need you above all things and desires. Walk with me beside this sea like you did with the fisherman you speak so lovingly about. Let me be like Esther when a life-and-death task was placed before her. She accepted peril and chose your purpose. Like her, give me the courage to say, "If I perish, I perish."

Let me prove true to you in my despair; let me trust you with the faith of Job; and then, Almighty God, please speak restoration into my life.

But like Job, I knew I had said enough already. God wasn't missing. God is never missing. Sometimes, though, I'm missing God.

Chapter 6
"THE DOCK WILL SEE YOU NOW"

When we got the news, we had already planned to go to Santa Barbara for Christmas. We weren't given much hope and at that time, there was no specific treatment for WM. We decided not to tell the kids; how tough that was, to keep it inside. Ken didn't want to upset their Christmas, so he decided to wait until after.

We were staying in a beautiful ocean-side hotel in Santa Barbara visiting with his sons, daughter, and in-laws, getting together either at their places or in our suite. They didn't have a clue, and as is typical with young people, they were all dealing with their own dramas at that time, so they were unaware. I felt like it was written all over my face. It was very sad in so many ways.

They had grown up with Beatles, movie stars, and famous cowboys around the house, and they loved having a dad who was invincible in their eyes. He wanted to keep their memories of the past in the present mode as much as possible. Ken will be the first to admit that this is not a good thing, but he liked keeping a certain image with his kids. They were not used to seeing him any other way.

—Connie

It turned out to be the middle part of the experience that occupied my mind when it came time to face my cancer. I didn't think about the end as much as I did about what was going on with God and me during that very unpleasant ordeal.

It was as if there were a short beginning to the whole experience: one day everything was normal, then I got the bad news. And the next day I was in the middle part—the part where I began fighting for my life. Suddenly everything had changed course, and the only clear message was there was to be no turning aside or away. I think the main thing that bothered me, though, was the lack of transition time.

I didn't like the sensation that I was being involuntarily ushered into a new phase in my life—one where I was being pushed out onto a stage where I didn't know my lines. There was no dress rehearsal. The show was going on the road, we were opening in Peoria, and my costume didn't fit.

I felt like the little kid in the story about a loving father who was sitting on the edge of a dock telling his son that he had to learn to swim to stay alive. Then, out of the blue, he pushed the boy off the dock into the lake. While he was in the air the young lad didn't spend a lot of time contemplating his options. While he was plunging beneath the surface, he wasn't thinking about how it was going to turn out, or even about dying. He spent his time trying to swim—fighting to stay alive and very much being "in the moment."

It would have been very hard in the middle of that frightening episode for the hapless kid to think in terms of learning or trusting or anything else having to do with organizing thoughts. His mind went into lockdown except for the immediate challenge before him. It all became very elemental; the focus was on simply getting through it.

A heavy cancer regime is also a sink-or-swim proposition. Like the struggling son in the water, I immediately lost a sense of what was up and down, and at what point I broke through the surface of my new reality into the place where I could breathe again. The sudden, extreme shift in priorities gave me a whiplash, but I was totally focused on the present of the trial; everything else was irrelevant. I found that the way to survive was to close my eyes, hold my breath, and wait until I floated to the surface. When I did that, when I became still, when I let go of what I do best (flailing around in my own efforts), then the waters became calm. That's when Jesus walked toward me on the surface of the lake and helped me get back to the safety of the dock.

I never said it was smooth sailing from that moment on, but I know now that I was not traveling alone. He spoke to me in the middle of my struggle, and his words were simple: "Be still, and know that I am God."[1] Those words carried me through the middle part of my ordeal, and I knew in my heart that they would stay with me to the end.

A very dear friend stopped by the house the other day to talk and announced that he was in deep trouble with a major cancer. He was starting chemo the next day and wanted my advice.

I told him three things: "Be still, know that he is God, and float!"

Chapter 7
KASS IN POINT

Ken's primary care doctor was incredible. She monitored his labs and encouraged him to see another oncologist after he had such a bad experience with the one in Santa Rosa, the one who gave the diagnosis, ordered the bone-marrow biopsy, and immediately set him up (or tried to) for a clinical trial that was incredibly invasive and extreme—heavy chemo time! I believe God gave Ken wisdom at that moment to say no. It turns out that particular protocol would have been very detrimental in the long run. He finally began seeing another oncologist late in 1997. His blood work was monitored every three to six months depending on the results.

—Connie

C ancer is very mysterious; it is also devious. It hides around dark corners, out of view. A neighbor, coworker, old classmate, or aunt Sara's ex-boyfriend are the ones who *have* it. It is fitting to feel sorry for a person who *has* it. It is my duty to pray for anyone I know who *has* it. It's wrong, but it's natural to consider it my good fortune that it is someone else who *has* it. Cancer is like a car wreck I read about that killed a bunch of kids on their way to a church youth retreat. *It is so heartbreaking that tragedy happened to those people, but those are misfortunes that would never occur in my world.* That's what I thought. It was so very, very strange to accept the fact that I was one of those people.

How could I face the unfamiliar world I was now occupying? I searched for answers but felt like someone had nailed my left big toe to the floor and I was just going around in bloody circles. When I eventually began to understand this situation, I was quite surprised at where my mind wandered. I traveled back to 1986, when cancer became more than a word to me. I now know how my friend Ron Kass felt, and I understand myself better as I look back on the first time I witnessed it happening to someone very important to me—someone who was a day-to-day, minute-to-minute person in my life.

Ron Kass was the president of Apple Records and one of the most special people I have ever known. He was my mentor, the person I looked up to the most, someone I respected and admired deeply. I never really understood what was actually going on in his life when he told me he had cancer.

He *had* cancer.

I knew having cancer was bad, but I was young and indomitable and had no idea of what was involved when someone *got* cancer. Ron was given six months to a year to live, and that was it—no cure, no treatment, and no hope. I couldn't accept that reality; something in me just could not absorb it.

A few months after Ron gave me the news, I flew to LA from Nashville to spend time with him. During my visit, I only saw the obvious aspects of the disease. He was much thinner, he moved excruciatingly slowly, and he talked softly as if it took great effort. Part of him was missing. I know now what was gone. Life had been draining out of him for months.

So there we were. I knew the mechanics. I should be kind and gentle because he had cancer. But I also knew that during our time together, it would be inappropriate to discuss it head-on. I had the feeling I get when someone dies and I am not quite sure how to act. How can I truly relate to death if I have never died? At the time, cancer, like being dead, was hard to understand because I had never been there.

As we talked, I became aware that my time was different from his time. I thought in terms of months, years, and weeks to come. His perceptions had to do with a dwindling amount of days with dwindling abilities. However, visiting someone you are close to, who is dying from cancer, is always the right thing to do. In Ron's case, it was also very proper. We were close friends, but not the crying-on-the-shoulder, let-it-all-hang-out kind of close. He was the absolute ruler of high-class protocol, and although the cancer had gotten the best of him, he remained in charge of the situation and surroundings. Because I was used to the way he handled circumstances, honoring this protocol was like hugging him. In spite of the ravages of the disease, he looked great and held court in dying as he did in living—in a suite at L'Ermitage Beverly Hills. As always, there were little finger foods to eat, placed artistically on porcelain plates along with champagne on ice, if one preferred.

It had all begun while we were in London. It was almost sixteen years after the Beatles' breakup and the closing of the doors of their business wild child, Apple Records. We were meeting there to see if we could revive the label with the original cast of characters. Ron called me in Nashville, filled me in on what he had been doing, and wanted to know if I could come to London to help him put it together. Before asking me to join him, he said he had been holding exploratory conversations with some of the Beatles, Yoko Ono, and major Apple staffers Derek Taylor, Neil Aspinal, Tony Bramwell, and Peter Asher. These get-togethers had gone well, although in a vaguely positive way. At the time, Ron had merely been on a fact-finding mission, but now it was time to take it to the next level, and he wanted me to join him before he put any more effort into the project.

The concept for reconstructing Apple would be to restart the company as an active label by staffing it only with the original members. That way it really would be Apple Records and not just some business venture. As America was still the most important market for the company's success, he felt that I, as the former US manager for the label, could help him concentrate our major relaunch efforts in that country, just as we had done with the original introduction of the enterprise. Although creatively inactive, Apple never did die, and to this day has not ceased being. But since its madness days at 3 Savile Row in London and eventual decline, Neil Aspinal had been saddled with the task of filing lawsuits against infringements on the Apple catalogue and copyrights, as well as managing the mass of assets the Beatles and their short venture had created. He confessed he was rather worn out with all the mundane aspects of his current responsibilities. Life at Apple had become admittedly quite different from the crazy days when the mop tops were raging and ruled the world.

Shortly after I arrived in London, Ron set up a luncheon at a restaurant on Baker Street with Neil and Tony Bramwell (the original promotion manager for the label), so we could begin taking a deeper look at the idea of bringing it back. With Ron Kass as the president, myself as the US manager, most of the main UK characters tentatively on board—including one-time international head and general manager Jack Oliver and a couple of the Beatles—we were well on our way. I brought an American investor with me who had agreed to underwrite the venture as the Beatles were not keen on going down that particular road again, the one with so many potholes and money pits. During the various meetings, it was so incredible to sit in familiar English pubs and private clubs with great friends, reliving one of the most exciting eras in the music business, having a couple of ales, and discussing the possibility of doing it all again. I was a little tired from jet lag at first, but as the venture began to look like a reality, my adrenaline began pumping full bore to the point I could have kick-started a 747 by the third day. My investor friend, who had made his fortune in vitamin supplements, was in awe and could not believe what he was experiencing.

But Ron had been acting strangely. He was constantly

excusing himself from our activities and important meetings. He would leave our table at restaurants for such long periods that his food would be cold by the time he returned. His demeanor was different than I remembered from the old days. There was an uncharacteristic moodiness about Ron that I had never witnessed before. He was also moving funny. When we would go for evening walks in Hyde Park after the day's business meetings, I would tease him that he was walking around so stiffly that it looked like the laundry had put too much starch in his shorts. Bramwell would jab Ron on the shoulder, exaggerate his Liverpool accent, and offer snide references suggesting that a strategically placed corncob was the reason he was walking so oddly.

Ron's strangeness was evolving into preoccupied remoteness and that was making it difficult to organize our plan of action. After a few days, we had gone as far as we could in our discussions with the British crew, so we left London with a list of items to think about and assignments to fulfill before we could proceed further. I was so jacked up with the possibility of polishing the Apple again that I could have flown back to Nashville without an airplane. I began immediately on my assignments. Upon returning to LA, Ron immediately went to see a doctor because he hadn't felt well during the London trip. They ran some tests and took some pictures. He called me with the news: they discovered a malignant cancerous tumor in his gut the size of a grapefruit.

We never discussed Apple again.

He died October 17, 1986—eight months after London. I didn't go to the funeral. I could not think of him that way.

I was having a hard time thinking of myself that way once

I received my diagnosis. Ron's ordeal had become the definitive version of the malady for me, even though I didn't understand it at the time. Over the years I have had many friends succumb to its terrors, but his was the face on the disease. His traumatic experience was the first time I encountered cancer. Then one day cancer was encountering me. My priorities were shifting so fast I had to carry a stopwatch and a notepad to keep track. I would think back on the waiting room of that cancer clinic in Santa Rosa, the one I visited when it all began. I wondered if I would wear a bandanna or would I wear my bald head like a badge of honor. Would I serve champagne as people watched me waste away? The things that kept haunting me were the words *incurable* and *no treatment*, plus the doctor's rather brief estimated timeline on my life. They used those words with Ron. Those were the words said to me. Would I see it through with the grace of my dear friend? Would I have eight months or eight years? Would I look as good as he did?

Would I have eight months or eight years?

Would I look as good as he did?

Chapter 8
CORNFLAKE CONFUSION

There was an experimental treatment in consideration, but nei-
ther Ken nor the doctor was anxious to give it a go. We felt
blessed that our new oncologist was cautious in the matter, and
together we decided upon a plan: we would not begin the experi-
mental treatment if the numbers from the regularly scheduled
lab tests were bad and Ken felt okay, or if Ken felt bad and the
numbers were okay. Here was our plan: when both the numbers
and Ken were looking bad, then we would go ahead and start
the experimental chemical therapy.

—Connie

C ancer is a battle within a battle. It's a battle that runs alongside a battle. It can even be a battle with God's Word when trying to understand how to fight things when he says that the battle belongs to him.

That's how the dialogue began between God and me over my morning cornflakes. I began to think, *These thoughts I'm having, are they conviction or condemnation? How am I supposed to feel when I am praying for the pain to go away and then the pain gets much worse?* Was that Satan condemning? Was it God convicting? Was it about God's love or correction? I became conflicted, and what really made it confusing was that I knew there is no conflict or confusion in God.

My health continued to worsen, and each day brought new discomfort. We began discussing the experimental treatment option with the oncologist. I understood that would put me in the middle of the middle, because once that process began, the treatment would have its own beginning and an end that would be inserted between diagnosis and eventuality.

I turned to God's promises and started a new conversation with him. As we talked, I began to find a peace with the trial— but then the sickness would skewer the senses. I struggled with his words, and because I didn't want to get mad, I began to pray. After a while I realized that was not working, because my words, my thoughts, and my emotions were becoming completely scattered, so I returned to asking him to alleviate the pain. Once again the pain got worse. By now I was totally adrift in all that drama. I found myself simply trying to pull all the pieces together—the promises and the pain, the Word and the worry, the Truth and the trial.

What happens to our bodies affects our minds and souls. God made us that way—that's why raising our hands in worship does something to our spirits, that's why kneeling in prayer affects our hearts. The chemically skewed reality that a cancer patient experiences is a living and dying thing that grates on his or her belief in God. I tried to pray, but I couldn't. I tried to hope, but the unrelenting discomfort prevailed.

Then there are those blissful souls who tell me about their "Damascus experience." For some reason they always make me feel as if I am not a real Christian, that maybe I am still that kid from the backwoods that would go into town and look into the candy-store window wishing I could have some. The analogy hurts because I never did get some of the sweet things of life until I struggled to get them. Finally, I just gave a piece of myself for them, just because I wanted to fit in.

My conversion to Christianity was the antidote to that sense of candy-store exclusion. People talk about coming to the Lord, but I always like to say that he came to me. In fact, I get the sense that he had been coming at me for years, in big chunks at times and other times in little sticky pieces—the kind that glom onto you whether you like it or not. It was like a quiet evolution, where one day I went from being a 49-percent Christian to a 50-percent Christian, and when I reached the 51-percent marker—I was one! From that point on, it was as though a barrier had been broken, and I was set free because I finally had an identity that fit. It was as if there were no numbers between 51 and 100. I was all in from that point on. I was no longer moving from belief system to belief system, or going from no system into just any system that felt good or finding one that gave me something vaporous to hang on to. Everything became so much clearer, and I loved the idea of thinking like a servant, moving simple love to the top of my list of priorities.

My confusion began to dissipate as soon as I realized that I had become so wrapped up in the overall cancer situation that I was overlooking its real purpose, which was my singular relational commitment with God the Father Almighty. It was actually about meditating on the meaning of those many moments that passed before my spiritual eyes and realizing that it all came down to my relationship with him. The discomfort was not a judgment against me—it was the means by which God shaped and defined me into the very image and likeness of his Son. I divinely understood that I was not to complain about my portion in the trial. I was not to murmur in my tent against the Lord, nor was I to question him or to rail out against my circumstances. Instead, I was to pray.

I was to pray for revelation.

I was to pray for those who didn't know how to pray.

I was to pray for those who didn't know whom to pray to.

I was to pray for those who didn't have anyone to pray for them.

I believe he was telling me that it had nothing to do with conviction, condemnation, correction, confusion, or cornflakes.

It had to do with caring.

His.

Chapter 9
THE OLD MAN AND THE C

There was no treatment until 2001. He had survived for five years since the 1996 diagnosis, beating the timeline odds but never feeling really good, and I felt that the Ken I used to know was gone in some ways. But he still had more energy than I did, and the most positive attitude that I've ever witnessed to this day. As the cancer progressed, I would spend longer times in prayer. He would take longer walks by the ocean. I would watch him from the living-room window as he slowly and deliberately picked his way over the dunes to reach the edge.

—Connie

As the cancer occupied more and more of my body, God occupied a greater percentage of my thoughts. It was becoming harder to get down to the sea and back home. The dunes were becoming an obstacle to getting to the edge. Connie thought I was taking longer walks—the truth is that it was taking me longer to walk. I was not as open as I used to be about my condition. I prayed more then. I ached all over, lived in constant pain, and when I got small cuts, I found ways to hide from her how much they bled.

It was a quiet morning. I was there at the water's edge earlier than usual. The new day glistened. I sensed his presence the minute I heard the breakers and their soothing rhythm. I no longer felt me—just him:

OH GOD, I LOVE YOU. I LOVE THE WAY YOU FILL MY thoughts, my very being. I especially treasure the times when you overwhelm me with your very presence. It amazes me every time I am amazed how you amaze me—it is amazing!

Today I am blessed with your wonder in the ocean, the sand, the sky, the very temperature that surrounds me. You fill me; you occupy me; you teach me; you heal me and guide me; you speak to me through your very Word.

I saw Peter as I watched the nets from the small fishing boats being emptied at a wharf off in the distance. How incredible it would have been to be one of those fishermen and have Jesus walk up and ask me to go with him, knowing that we would be speaking the words of eternal salvation into lives for generations to come. To those undeserving, odd souls like me, truly longing for that unknown truth that only Jesus can reveal. I wondered if I would have dropped everything and gone with him. I feared that I would cling to the worldly nets that engulfed me. I feared that I would hesitate to make the sacrifice he required. He asks that we lay down our lives for him—and I still worry about what I am going to wear each day.

I tried to picture my reaction to a gentle man who would have approached me on the shore and asked me to commit my life to him, to give up my family and my whole existence as I had known it. Knowing me, I would have been intrigued by his open simplicity and boldness of purpose. I wished I could see his face as those fishermen saw it on that day. I wished I could have known him then. I wished he were here with me in that form that day. I wished I would only believe him better than I did!

Oh God, I love you. Look at me across this ocean before me and touch me, heal me, put your arms around me and draw me into your Way and your Will and your Word. Oh how I long to swim out to you and drink of your living water—water you can walk on—water I can depend on—the water that will support and cleanse me. Oh God, I love you!

I turned to walk up from the beach to the house. I wished I could call Connie to come and get me. I had been carrying that dread and that disease for so long. It had finally become heavier than I could bear. I didn't want to go into treatment. I had heard so many horror stories, but my hesitancy was fading in relationship to the way I felt. I knew that I couldn't hide how bad it was getting from Connie anymore.

Chapter 10
PAST, PRESENT, FUTURE

Five years had gone by, and we were still struggling with the situation but had found a place of acceptance in dealing with the cancer. In February 2001 we went to San Francisco on business, and late one evening, Ken's nose started bleeding. It didn't stop, and blood was everywhere. He felt he could get it under control, so I did not call 911 when I should have. I waited too long, and hopefully I will never do that again. He stuffed his nose with tissues, but eventually it was pouring out of his mouth. I finally did call around eleven at night. He was so embarrassed to have the paramedics come to our room and carry him and his bloody face out through the lobby of a very nice San Francisco hotel on a gurney in his pj's.

I rode in the cab of the ambulance to a hospital in the Castro district. It was surreal and very frightening to have this happen, let alone while we were away from home. The doctor on duty did some things in his nose, put what looked like a Tampax up his left nostril, and sent us back to the hotel in a cab around three or four in the morning. It took that long! We were exhausted and fell asleep immediately—but the phone rang at 5:30 a.m. and woke us up. It was one of my girlfriends from Nashville who had forgotten about the time change. I could have strangled her! Ken, with no sleep, a swollen face, and stuff sticking out of his nose, insisted on completing our business that morning before driving back to Bodega Bay and seeing our regular doctor on the way home.

Results from recent blood work were dangerously out of normal range and were climbing. This occurrence turned out to be a symptom of WM. All the years leading up to this, there were the symptoms—joint pain, weakness, brain fog, bleeding that was hard to stop, being sick or just not feeling good, and various physical discomforts that were hard to define. He knew he was deteriorating in a general sense; and in my simple way, I just wanted him to feel better.

—Connie

n addition to the physical distress WM was causing, it also made me feel stupid. This is a common aspect of the disease. I found it hard to think through things. As the organization of data became more difficult, something interesting was happening: my God-thoughts took over with a comforting simplicity and ease. Many times when I was tired, though, my mortal thoughts crept in and took center stage.

I spent most of my adult life on the road, but the cancer trip was taking me on an inner journey that was not easy to pack for. On an earthly level, I felt as if I was losing my identity. When I didn't know what was before me, when I couldn't make plans, when I didn't have a place to put myself in the worldly scheme of things, I ceased being able to see myself.

My identity was wrapped up in three things: my past, my present, and my future. I knew where I had been, I knew where I was in the present, and up until that point I'd had a basic idea of where I was going. That was my uniqueness; that was me: a mortal projectile careening across the earth at warp speed, flying low, glancing nervously in my soul's rearview mirror at the years in my past.

At the same time, I was watching my current movements in the reflections of people's eyes as I made my way along God's path, trying to stay relevant and on course in my walk in the Word. Simultaneously, I was always looking ahead as I plunged helter-skelter into my remaining time on earth. But incurable cancer? I no longer had a sense of who I was, because I couldn't see where I was going. Those were my natural thoughts, but when I pulled my head out of the muck and looked to the heavens, I remembered that I was God's child and, in his eternal plan, all I had to do was trust in him. But there I was, and it wasn't that easy.

I knew treatment was just around the corner, so that particular philosophical dialogue expanded. I admit that I was trying to hide out inside my head where no one could find me. There is a lot of room in there, so to make sense of things I tried to break it down and further examine these pieces: past, present, and future, and my place in them.

THE PAST?

I have always said that because we are made up of our past, present, and future, that if one of these is missing, then so are we. Then the cancer came, and I suddenly became an altered being; everything about my past became suddenly unimportant.

I always looked forward to getting older. I imagined the peace and serenity of that age when everything would be quiet and in order. I didn't realize that it would hurt so much. The only thing these days that doesn't hurt in my body is my appendix, which was removed when I was in college. I know now that I blew it. In my rock-and-roll youth, I always operated under the knowledge that if I was cautious with my finances, relationships, and plans for the future, I might have security, but then I didn't want to miss all the excitement, travel, and fascinating people I met. I gladly traded pensions, homes, and retirement plans for the memories of an incredibly spectacular life that only few can imagine. I thought I was invincible. Maladies, setbacks, calamities, cancer—me? Never! The problem is that as I get older, my memory is fading and I am having a hard time remembering all those good times!

My good memories meant nothing because of the state I was in. My accomplishments, lessons learned, victories achieved, and fond reflections of past events began to feel like a waste of time. The way I felt dissolved all that I was; everything that had led up to that moment in time was wiped out by that very moment. It didn't matter how I got there—I was in this place, and it occupied 100 percent of my being. It all boiled down to one thing: my past has passed and whatever happened in that past had passed away. So where did that leave me?

The Future?

Forget about those glamorous thoughts of the future, the house on the lake, the trip to Tuscany, the new grandchildren, and the hike on the Appalachian Trail. I couldn't see beyond the discomfort long enough to have an imagination or a semblance of hope. Even mustering up a decent prayer became close to impossible at times. One reason it was so hard to envision the future was that I was not sure I was going to be there, so I ended up getting lost within the vapor of trying to put a face on it. Talk about looking in a mirror darkly. My body chemistry was changing, and my mind was not excused from the process. Worse, even if I could get past that vacuum and was able to look ahead (what if there was to be a cure?), I didn't have a clue what kind of shape I was going to be in.

Would I be able to enjoy the future or even participate in its motion? Would I be so destroyed physically that I would either be unable to take part in the events or feel good enough to appreciate them? Would I be unable to generate the income to have an operational future, or would the potential financial outcome drive me into poverty, which made the whole thing feel fruitless anyway?

What about Connie? Do not get me started on how her future weighed on me. We Christians have these thoughts right along with everyone else, even though we have all the answers in our well-worn Bibles. Yes, we have faith; yes, we have hope; yes, we have God's promises. Yes, we have cancer.

THE PRESENT?

I have always been told to live in the present. I tried to take a positive spin on the ordeal as it began unfolding and thought how great it would be to be able to take advantage of the downtime. I thought about all the time I was going to have to read, study my Bible, and to spend in positive communication with my Lord and Savior. Well, that wasn't happening. It hurt to read, the promises in the Word hurt, and watching those sinners frolicking on the beach on TV really hurt.

In that present time, I was stripped of my appetite, of my strength, of my passions, and most of my mental acuteness. Without the past and the future in play, I became like a three-legged stool with only one leg. I lost my balance. I toppled under the weight. Most of the time I had only one thing going: feeling each agonizing minute slowly drift into the next one. A single thought occupied my mind: Was the next minute going to be better or worse?

Though this thought process may seem devoid of hope and faith in God, like mere animal survival, this was still a spiritual battle. It is easy to have faith, be faithful, and to be the personification of faith when everything is going okay, but it was from the dark hole that cancer dug that I discovered that faith was the rope I needed to grab on to in order to pull myself out. I needed to rise above the lies and the torments from the devil, who told me that even with faith I was doomed.

I finally wised up, told the devil to go to hell where he belonged, and thanked God that I had had a past, that he was with me in the present, and most of all, that I knew what his future held in store. King David had thoughts like those, so I found comfort knowing that he was a man after God's own heart. I knew that anyone who had been in the depths of a rugged battle, cancer or otherwise, has felt that way at some time.

Think about this: With God there is no past, present or future. He is the *I Am*. He always has been and forever will be. His time is eternity, which has no beginning, phases, or finality. After I finished wallowing in those doubting thoughts for a while, I eventually brought it all to the One who has all the answers—and the One to whom I ultimately answer.

I read *The Living Bible* as my main devotion because that is the version Connie gave me when she was witnessing to me about the Lord. It is amazing how God works; now we have a traveling ministry and are on the road speaking at churches and events about 50 percent of our time. I never take that Bible with me on the road. I don't ever want to lose it. I use the ones in the hotel nightstands. Sometimes at home, I will just grab it and hold on to it very tight without opening it; it is such a comfort to me. It has me all over it and in it—tearstains, torn leaves, underlines, and peanut butter smudges. In fact, because I've showered and shaved before doing my devotions for so many years, it smells like my shaving lotion.

One day while I was struggling with God, he reminded me of something from those worn pages that put it all in a proper perspective for me. It was a cloudy day outside and an even darker one inside, and everything seemed so hopeless. I was completely discouraged. I felt he was letting me down, and I told him so in clear and precise terms. In the midst of reviewing my hopeless past-present-future routine, a simple thought stopped me in my tracks. He began speaking to me. The message was clear, lifted me out of my hole, and sat me on solid ground: "Don't get mad at the only one who can help you."

I was not mad at God. I know that. Maybe I thought I was, but in fact, I was not mad at all. I simply did not like what was going on within my body. With each passing moment, I found it harder to ignore the signs. It was also becoming more difficult to do the things I had to do to live a normal life. The toughest thing was to see Connie picking up the heavier end of the load we shared as a husband and wife. I knew she knew I was faking it when I told her I was doing okay. We had been told from the start that it was a slow-moving cancer; so, much to her dismay, I might have been taking things a bit too slow as far as facing my reality.

Chapter 11

ON THE ROAD AGAIN

Ken's IgM kept rising, and he was feeling crappier all the time, gaining a lot of weight as well. That was really hard for him because Ken had always worked really hard at staying healthy and in shape. His immune system was fighting so hard that his metabolism had basically stopped. He had no strength or energy—therefore the weight gain.

My fiftieth birthday was in June 2001, and Ken started early asking me where I wanted to go—anywhere in the world, Italy, you name it. I instinctively knew that we should stay close to home. Through our business, I was able to get a guesthouse at Beaulieu Vineyards, which felt like it could be somewhere in Italy. A beautiful, 10,000-square-foot, Frank Lloyd Wright—style home with a picturesque, wisteria-lined veranda overlooked the mountains and out across vineyards. Stunning. We had it all to ourselves.

In addition, Ken called Mike Benziger, who gave us the guesthouse at Benziger Vineyards for the night before my birthday, so we had two nights away in wine country. Ken surprised me with a birthday cake at each place, and his daughter gave me a spa certificate for the day of my actual birthday.

We had a doctor's appointment the day before we left, and that's when we learned Ken needed to have treatment. Denial was no longer an option, at least for me. It cast a dark shadow over the getaway. Knowing we were going to be celebrating my fiftieth was especially hard for me because I knew Ken was determined to celebrate in style regardless of the news.

It was a slightly rainy day in Napa Valley, and Ken had booked the Napa Wine Train tour for lunch. It was so strange to sit there across from each other, knowing—not knowing—what was ahead. I wanted to cancel the spa treatment, but he insisted. As I was lying there, tears just poured out of me as the massage therapist treated me. She never asked why.

We decided to go ahead with the new experimental treatment for WM that was having success with other blood cancers. It is called Rituxan. It is a target-cell therapy, without so many of the nasty side effects of hard-line chemo.

—Connie

t felt so odd to be sitting in a room with a bunch of strangers; we all had bags hanging overhead with tubes coming down and ending under strips of tape on our arms. I looked up; the liquid looked so innocent as it drip-drip-dripped.

In some ways, it wasn't as bad as I expected, the four weeks of chemical therapy. If you don't count the first week or so. Connie drove me to the clinic on Tuesday mornings, and I spent most of the day receiving the infusions. The length of the day depended on how fast I could absorb the fluids. Most of the time I got very bad chills, to the point that they had to shut down the valve for a while. The first week following the injections, I had a rough time with fevers and chills. One night I became so sick that she wanted to drive me to the emergency room. Each week it got better, though, so by the end of the month I was handling the invasions like a pro. Being able to look out from our home on the bay at the pelicans diving for fish while the seals barked and played around the fishing boats coming in and out of the harbor was definitely the way to go when going through that process. Outside my window was good—but what was going on inside my body seemed foreign to me, especially the strange taste in my mouth.

I had many hours to study myself during the days following the therapy, and I was learning that it was not the trial that ran me off God's highway but my reaction to it. How I handled it. I knew from experience that when I started questioning what

God was up to, it automatically put the brakes on my spiritual journey. When that happened, I would pull over to the side of the road and get out my God map, the Bible. If I believed he was the Way, the Truth, and the Life, why would I choose any other route than the one he laid out for me? After spending time in his Word, the journey became clearly defined. The question was, do I travel with faith or fear as my companion?

Faith means I believe that God can handle a situation, and fear says he cannot. Faith is telling God that I trust him in all things and believe every word he says is true. Fear is calling God a liar! I love it when God spoke to the prophet Isaiah about this. He said it about as well as it can be said: "Woe to the man who fights with his Creator."[1]

Dealing with cancer is just one of the many things I could face in my journey. When trials and tragedies strike, it isn't the nature of the actual incident that is of import. In fact, what gives a trial its value is its unpredictability; it can be any kind of event. As a Christian, I am left with fewer options than I had as an unbeliever when facing a new crisis. I now have only two: trust God or don't trust God.

It took what seemed to be an eternity of repeatedly telling myself that I was going to trust him for me to get to the point where I actually began trusting him. The transition of trying to apply my faith and having it kick in was like sipping sweet well water. First, there was that great thirst, and then—ah!—righteous refreshment! Like the water from the well, an incredible calm and beauty filled me when I realized how delicious it was to experience the fantastic truth that God was all I truly needed. It was like a cool breeze on a warm day when that empty space inside became filled completely with his love and his promises. Nothing really mattered; worldly weights faded away, leaving behind all that really counts—his mercy, grace, and unfailing love.

Once I left my worldly desires, I was no longer driving aimlessly; the destination was clearly in sight—my oneness with him. I confessed that it had all gone beyond me. I got to be a child again, and my worn outside was replaced by a warm inside heated by his all-consuming fire. My circumstances were out of my control, so I just trusted my Father and no longer worried about the illness and issues that were before me.

Those were my thoughts that final day in the room at the oncology clinic when abruptly, and out of my mist, I heard the beeper go off. The infusion was finished for that week. The nurse unplugged the bag, removed the needle from my arm, and sent me on *his* way.

Chapter 12
MY SWEET GEORGE

Ken finished his last treatment on September 10, 2001. He had a rough beginning but tolerated it very well overall. The next day we decided to take an early-morning walk out on Bodega Head—the morning of September 11. Who can forget exactly what they were doing that morning? It was one of the most spectacularly sunny and clear mornings we had ever seen on the north coast, and we could see forever at the cliff's edge of the Pacific. We were both surprised at how quiet it was and how we were the only ones there. We stopped and gave thanks for the beauty and peace in that place, not having a clue what had or was happening in New York City. We went back home, and Ken decided to stay there to rest and write while I went to work.

I opened our seaside shop, Gourmet Au Bay, at 11:00 a.m., and once everything was in place, I made a call to one of our vendors in Canada to place an order. She informed me that our borders were closed. That's when I learned about 9/11. I immediately called Ken, and he turned on the TV for the first time that day and saw the news.

Everything was different from that point on. Three months slipped by as we became lost in the daze of what had happened to our country and the daze of wondering if the treatment had worked.

—Connie

S ummer was a bummer because of the treatments. A couple of months had gone by since the final one, and it was late November, a vibrant time on the north coast of California. Vacationers from all over the world would flock to our shores during the summer months, but after Labor Day, the number of visitors dwindled. Locals were left blissfully alone except for a few romantic couples or retirees who ventured a visit in their motor homes.

The funny thing is that the weather during the tourist season is mainly foggy, windy, and cold. September, though, is when it starts getting dramatically beautiful along the edge. October and November are even more stunning, but life is different on the north coast of California, and it does take a certain kind of person to be moved by the uniqueness of that special place. The year-round cold water makes it almost too cold to swim in the ocean. As striking as the beaches are there, many tourists are disappointed in their visits. Most visitors become chilled, buy a movie poster of *The Birds* or an Alfred Hitchcock sweatshirt, and sit in the bar at the Tides Wharf complaining about the wind. We would tell them that we call our little town "Blowdega Bay," and that we dig the way the wind and fog make our hair do funny things.

Bodega Bay is a hearty place with its turbulent ocean and

unpredictable weather, but that is what makes it so special. Any given day of the year can be the most spectacular day on earth. The bad weather sets the good weather up, and in time, it becomes such an integral part of the beauty that to have it any other way would be a disappointment.

I came to that little fishing village to live because I liked being in an intermediate place—a place that existed between an inner turbulence that kept me on my feet and a distant quiet that forced me to move at a liquid, slow pace. I liked the small number of people living there and the fact that those who did kept to themselves. So many years of being in crowds and having to be "on" left me a bit reclusive by choice. So Bodega Bay was where I landed as I approached my sixties. The time had come to unpack my tattered baggage and unload my crumpled stuff *from* the sixties.

Anytime the phone rings after 10:00 p.m., my gut tightens up, no matter where I am. No one typically calls during that time unless it's important, and if it is important good news, then they usually wait until morning. I was especially unnerved on a late-November Friday morning in 2001 when a call came in somewhere around three thirty in the morning. There was no caller ID on our bedroom phone back then, but I was afraid to ignore it—even more afraid of what it might be about. I answered, and it wasn't good news.

George Harrison had passed away at 1:30 the preceding afternoon at a private residence in LA. His wife, Olivia, and son, Dhani, withheld the news of his death until midnight California time, at which time the information was released worldwide. When the world did find out, Olivia and Dhani had already held a quiet funeral service with a very select group of close friends.

They had cremated his body, all according to George's wishes. At midnight they were secluded from the media, traveling on a private jet on its way to India, where the ashes were to be spread on the Ganges river according to Hare Krishna traditions.

What this meant was that the networks on the East Coast did not become aware of this "big story" until 3:00 a.m. EST, and they began scrambling. It didn't take Fox News long to come up with my name for their segments on the "quiet" Beatle, as I had appeared on the network several times in the past for related Fab-Four happenings.

My predawn disturbance was New York calling to interview me and also to find out if they could arrange for me to come to their studios in San Francisco for live in-person interviews. In addition to an on-the-spot predawn telephone interview, they wanted me to appear on three different shows that day starting with their morning news anchors. I think the reason Fox News liked having me as a guest is because there are not very many of us who were with the Beatles who (a) were still alive and (b) could speak in complete sentences.

George had died from cancer. Coincidently, I was scheduled for an important 9:00 a.m. meeting with my oncologist in Sebastopol, California, that very morning. We had planned to go over recent blood tests to find out if the August-September treatments had worked. The fear of bad news had kept me up that night, which made me less than cordial to their intrusion and requests. I refused the on-the-spot phone interview (I was lying in bed, half asleep, for crying out loud!) and delayed agreeing to do their on-camera interviews until after my doctor's appointment that morning. Obviously, I never did go back to sleep, and the day was starting out very badly.

I was very nervous about my morning meeting with the oncologist. George's passing had put a different face on the reality of my situation, and in a way, it replaced the one gathered from Ron Kass because of its immediacy. Our cancers were vastly different—his was lung cancer, and mine was taking place in my bone marrow. It had been three months since I completed chemical therapy, and, unfortunately, I was not doing well. The reason for this appointment was not only to review the results of the medical tests in order to determine if I had responded to the regime, but also to plan on how to proceed in the future. Connie and I had been praying faithfully for a successful outcome to the experimental treatment; being told eleven months ago that I had only one to three years to live, was a little unsettling. Time could be running out.

I have a great relationship with the people at Fox, and Connie and I have become friends with two of the anchors there. The problem that day was that the fast-action people responsible for putting show content together kept calling us every half hour, trying to get a commitment from me to do the shows they had planned. The quickest I could get to their studios in San Francisco was about an hour and a half with good traffic, so they needed to plan ahead. They had my phone numbers logged in their address files, so the calls continued to our cell phone after we left the house and were on our way inland to the doctor's office. I was honored by the invitations but also bugged by the aggressiveness that was invading my mission to find out about my own life-threatening situation.

We arrived at the oncologist's office on time. After a short wait, I was ushered into an unfamiliar room—not an examination room but an office with a cluttered brown desk and a wall lined with diplomas and certificates. It was obviously his private office. I had never been in this room before, so that was my first clue that the news was not going to be good. Meanwhile, Connie was out in the waiting room pacing the floor and fielding calls from the media. She was extremely worried about what was going on with me and becoming very annoyed with the calls that had escalated to one every few minutes. She would not give them an answer until she talked to me. The powers that be at Fox finally decided that because of schedules and the distance I would have to travel to get to their studios, they would send a car to our house in case I agreed to do the interviews. She told them to go ahead, and we would just send it back if I decided not to come. That was fine with them; they finally quit calling.

My test results were not good. The oncologist's initial take on the numbers on the lab sheets coupled with my worsening condition led him to believe that the treatment had failed. In summary, he felt there was not much that could be done about my situation. Although there was no big hurry, he suggested that in the coming months it would be a good idea to "get our affairs in order."

Such a dainty little phrase: "getting our affairs in order." It almost made me want to write a song with that title—something like "Staying Alive" from *Saturday Night Fever*—you know, something you can dance to!

> *Everybody's dancin'*
> *Everybody's prancin'*
> *Gittin' our affairs in order . . .*
> *Affairs in order*

The guys er all playin'
The girls er all prayin'
Gittin' our affairs in order . . .
Affairs in order

Ah Ah Ah Ah
Affairs in order
Affairs in order

Ah Ah Ah Ah
Affairs in order
Affairs in order
Affairs in orderrrrrrrr—yeah

When I came out to the lobby, it took Connie less than a nanosecond to know what the results were. We are so close that our deep understanding of each other tends to negate the need for dialogue in important situations. When heavy stuff happens, it is almost as if we feel we need to be quiet so we can sense how our hearts are beating and get them synced up. It reminds me of an incredible lyric from a Jessi Colter song on an album I once produced for Capitol Records: "Speak softly, move slowly. Great moments always scare me!" We have learned over the years that great, scary moments do have to be approached cautiously, especially when we may soon be "gittin' our affairs in order . . . affairs in order."

We drifted out to the parking lot, settled into the car, and headed for home. We cleared the outskirts of the little town where the hospital is located, and as soon as it was mostly trees and a few houses flashing by the windows, I repeated to Connie what the oncologist had told me. Because we had been given no concrete options at this point, the word *incurable* seemed to drown out the moment. There was not much to talk about. We had covered this ground before. It was then that she told me about Fox News and the limo that would be waiting for us when we arrived at our house. To her great surprise, I said I wanted to do the shows.

I had a very special relationship with George over the years, and I wanted to do this for him. My decision not only had to do with paying my respects and showing my appreciation for how good he had been to me, but I also understood the battle he had just lost. We were comrades in arms, the magic of our youth and trials of the later years creating an odd, minor-key bond between us. I also wanted to get away from my ordeal and think about someone else for a change.

The interviews went great, and it was also fun sharing with people what George Harrison was like in real life. My daughter was on a business trip in the city that day and was not only able to join me for some of the shows but decided to ride with us back to Bodega Bay. I appeared on three Fox shows live in the studio, and I also gave a live CBS phone interview during the ride home in Fox's limo. I felt good about the day, and the high activity schedule watered down my tribulation.

I thought I had done this for George, but actually, once again, he had done a favor for me in his soft, gentle way. I fell asleep that night knowing that he and I had our affairs in order.

Chapter 13
BLINDED BY THE LIGHT

As it turned out, due to the newness of the experimental treatment, even Ken's oncologist didn't know that it was not uncommon to have what is known as a "Rituxan flare" when the IgM number goes up instead of down as it should for a period of time after the treatment.

I'm not sure when we all learned about the flare oddity, but Ken did begin feeling better, and his numbers started dropping the following spring.

WM is still considered an orphan cancer—one that strikes a very small percentage of the population. The good news is that it has finally garnered attention, and research is making great advances in treating this disease, though it remains incurable. I still get nervous every time we go to the oncologist (every three to six months, depending on his symptoms and/or his IgM number).

Each time he has his blood drawn, I ask God to please deliver him from this and all cancer, and that he would send his healing balm through Ken's bloodstream. Because of the increased interest and extensive research, the statistics have changed since we first learned of this unwelcome guest; the life expectancy now surpasses ten years.

—Connie

Some call it blind faith, usually in a critical tone of voice, when responding to a devoted Christian expressing the basis of his or her belief. They tend to use a certain tone and accompanying body language when they say that phrase, making it sound like a Christian's blind faith is a bad thing.

Here's how I see it. The Bible tells me that Jesus is the light of the world, and I know that his love, mercy, and grace shine so brightly that when we draw close to him, an obvious result for the true follower is to be blinded by "the Light." Maybe it's because the experience is so beautiful; the reason we can't see is that we have closed our eyes in exultation and are luxuriating in his gorgeous wonder. In all this loveliness though, there can be a shiny downside to being a true follower.

Paradoxically, as I shed the junk in my life and draw closer to the Light, the closer I get, the more "stuff" I begin to see. This may sound discouraging, but I find that God is very patient. He knows me so well; he knows that if he turned up the light real bright all of a sudden and brought it real close, so I could become totally aware of all my shortcomings at one time, then I would be totally blown away. I would be overwhelmed by what I would see in myself.

Maybe this is why they call the Christian life a "walk." We have to take it one step at a time once we are put on track. If I want to go to Des Moines, Iowa, from Bodega Bay, California, I can not just "be there" all at once. There are steps to take and things to accomplish along the way to get me there. There will be mountains to go over and valleys to rest in along the way.

I notice that as my walk matures, I love its learned simplicity. After facing and surviving the contrasting, cruel darkness of a cancer battle, I no longer try to think through things so deeply. Once I strip down for the fight and shed the importance of so many worldly attachments, I discover a certain peace in the eye of the storm—once I enter the realm of his love and compassion.

It's not all fluffiness on my spiritual cloud. I confess there are times that I can't get my harp to stay in tune and my spiritual virtuosity falls into the category of, "what did I do that was so bad in my life to make me deserve this?" It is almost impossible to avoid going there at least for a little while, even though I have to leave God's truth to get there. This is known as the "God of Wrath" path as opposed to the "God is Love" path.

One very dark night, I got into one of those mind warps. I was born and blessed with a near-genius IQ—a fact discovered when I joined the navy. During the enlistment process, I kept scoring so high on various exams and tests that they called another fellow and me into a separate room. They had us take what they called a GCT—the navy's version of an IQ test. The next day they gave us the news that we were much smarter than most—an "in the top 5 percent" rating, I believe was the phrase. They then invited us to make the US Navy a career. We were informed that in all the years the navy had been giving that battery of tests, this other fellow and I were the first and only recruits up to that point to score a perfect 100 on the main test. I had just turned eighteen a few weeks before.

I left that room armed with this information and used it to

walk over, do in, outdo, overcome, go over, go beyond, move to the front of, and outdistance anyone or anything that got in my way, stood in my way, or was encountered along the way. It was this gift that got me to where I was later in life: successful and messed up! I was a smart kid, and I thought I had something to do with that—not a loving heavenly Father who had truly blessed me with certain talents and abilities. I could have used this asset in many ways, but the world salutes those who take advantage of blessings of this sort. I found that one of the manifestations of this gift could be the art of manipulation, deception, and unfair advantage.

The problem is, when the cancer came and I was no longer in control, I found myself at an obvious disadvantage. For the first time, I couldn't finagle myself out of a situation. On my back with the lights long turned off, I was feeling sicker than a cross-eyed dog with the whooping cough when I finally weakened. I slowly began sorting through the pieces from my darkened past, and then embarked on a guilt trip. My reasoning was that if I was the one who made me so smart, then it had to be me and my sin that made me so sick.

Following this mind-bend was the beginning of a journey into a deep hole—a descent that started with me ignoring the fact that I have been totally forgiven for all the bad moves I made in the past. I was now cave diving into that aspect of my life and trying to slather as much pit slime on it as I possibly could.

The dark thoughts gathered momentum. *Was my inconsideration of my fellow man the deed that brought me to my great punishment? Was it the inherent sex, drugs, and rock and roll that so naturally came from my success that put the final kibosh on a trial-free life for all time?*

I know now that I didn't go to this dark place alone. Nor was I the first one to explore that deep space. Many have traveled there before me, and, sadly, many poor souls suffering in the throes of the cancer fight will follow. The truly heart-wrenching ones are those who don't know the Lord and therefore don't eventually pull themselves out of the abyss when they see the light of the Son shining in. It can be a bottomless pit unless we have a Savior who yanks us out of there by reaching down with nail-scarred hands—a lifter of our souls. For me it was in these darkest of dark places that the light became most apparent. Even a tiny little light is noticeable in a dark place like that. It is this light that leads us out as our thoughts once more go above ground.

When I became a Christian, I knew I needed to take my head out of a holey place and have it be in a holy place—one that lives, dwells, and has its good purpose in my heart. Simply being in his presence is the way I experience my greatest and most illuminating moments with the Lord. It is that special moment when something unexplainable but very recognizable comes over my being, that I rise up out of the abyss as his tender compassion fills the air. I find supreme joy in those moments when a sense of warmth and love wash over me and into me, and I discover there are no words to describe it. It is his light shining into my darkness. That is when I know his gentle arms are around me, letting me know he is there.

A special tranquility takes place in this scenario. There are no subtitles needed to round out the picture. It is a "knowing that I know" kind of thing. It becomes personal and ethereal, that God-to-man, man-to-God moment. It allows me to love the Lord with all my being. He honors me with his perfect time and gracious touch during those moments when I need a hug. My thoughts return to him and his promises, mercy, and grace, and I become thankful for the special feeling we share.

I finally put the pieces together concerning this impression one quiet day as I walked along the water's edge, praying during the end part of my Bodega Bay bout with cancer. I was finally over the hump, and it was good to have the strength to get out and smell the sea air. I was thankful and blessed to be out in the open again. It was an exceptionally clear day, and the setting sun was approaching the distant sea edge. It was so dazzling as it bounced off the water that its brilliance and the shimmering sea were all I could see. I stopped, facing westward, blinded by the light of his creation. God saw my joy as I covered my eyes, gazed across the water, and searched the horizon. He asked me if I could ever love anything more than I love the ocean. I thought about it for a moment and then said, "Yes, but only if it was bigger and more beautiful."

He said, "Thank you," and hugged my heart.

BETWEEN THE CRACKS

We moved temporarily to Santa Rosa in February 2002, and by April, I remember Ken coming inside from sunning himself on our patio and exclaiming, "I cannot believe how good I feel." I was thrilled. Could it be that our lives could be normal again? We left for Hawaii a couple of months later to housesit for some dear friends for six weeks. It was luxurious. Ken was writing, I read books, we went to the beach a lot, and we ate at local restaurants. We had fresh papaya right off the trees in the yard every morning for breakfast. I attribute that to improving health for both of us. I'll never forget that taste!

Even though the WM was still there, we put it on the back burner for a while. There were times when Ken still "didn't feel great," as he is fond of saying, but our lives were somewhat normal, healthwise. He still had to be monitored every six months with blood analysis and physical exams, something the WM docs call "watch and wait." It's an indolent cancer and it can lay low or make its move; it's hard to say and it's not very clear. Unlike so many other diseases that have specific symptoms and specific treatment protocols, WM is elusive.

Without asking us our opinion about what we wanted to do next with our lives, God moved us into an exciting traveling ministry at that time. It was rough at first because the ordeal had taken a toll, and Ken had barely begun regaining his strength. It amazes me that he always has the might to give his all when the time comes, even if he is feeling ill before, during, and after. We knew in looking back over the road we had traveled during that rough journey that God had been with us the whole time, so it was only logical he would be with us during the physical travels that lay ahead.

—Connie

Dealing with cancer is not as linear as most books describe the ordeal. Going into it, going through it, and coming out of cancer is not that orderly. The battle is more of a hanging on, a falling apart, a sense of loss, and a lot of lonely flailing among the rubble. Believers are given the scripted message that cancer is a godly adventure and that it only hurts for a little while—that there is a shiny reward for the faithful at the end. The rubber-meets-the-road reality of the tale is that it hurts! You are never in the end when you are going through it—you are in it, that lonely middle part, and its terrors are coming down right now! The truths of God's living Word and the confused sufferer's life of pain seem to pile up on opposite sides of the scrambled mess once called a belief system. It is that in-between place that drives a person crazy—a between-the-cracks spot that everyone can identify with, whether they are suffering cancer or not. It's where David lived in some of the psalms. It's where Moses lived in the desert. It's where all of us live at some point in time, and it's where we meet God in the most real, visceral way.

Book Two

CALAVERAS COUNTY, CALIFORNIA, 2009–2012

Chapter 13
WALLY

I n 2002 God moved us from Santa Rosa to a new and special place, a few hours away from the ever-present sea in our lives. We felt as though we had nothing to do with leaving the edge. It was as if one day we woke up to discover that we had been deposited upon the foliage-heavy foothills of the magnificent Sierra Nevada mountains—two blessedly entwined souls gathered up from the eternal tides of our coastal years and swept eastward across California's fertile valleys onto a new edge—a mountain edge, an elevated soft edge where we were to be properly nestled in our Father's constant and ever-loving arms.

It is gold country, wine country, rolling foothill country— and most of all, just plain country. We needed a change. The years of dealing with WM were behind us. In their place came a different setting, and a different momentum in the form of a traveling ministry that has taken over our lives. We soon discovered it was easier to travel from our home in the mountains because it's a straight shot to the Sacramento International Airport instead of the long, complicated, highly unpredictable drive from Bodega Bay, through crowded Marin County and San Francisco's congested city streets, and then onto the freeway heading south to SFO International Airport.

Even with the complications of "life on the road" back in our lives, living has become much simpler. We explore the Sierra Nevada foothills, walk high mountain trails, and kick back when we are home. Most of the time though, we travel the back roads and major highways of the Northwest or the vast expanse of California, speaking at churches. As the years since the treatment for WM have passed by, we have learned to let life unfold before us—one that we are not quite sure we completely understand. Once or twice a month this westerly rhythm is broken by the discomfort of eastbound airplanes, west–of-the-Rockies appearances, and enough hotel stays to classify us as Diamond Elite status with the Hilton family of hotels.

Connie makes sure I pay attention to the semiannual hospital visits needed for the uncomfortable tests that were prescribed to keep an eye out for Wally's potential return. We began calling WM "Wally" over the years, because Waldenström's macroglobulinemia is so hard to work into a conversation. I used to think I would probably die from WM before I would learn to pronounce it. In the early years, when the cancer would really take me down and drain me of my strength, I would joke that I had hit the "Wally."

Something inside of me chooses to ignore the fact that there is an illness that still lingers deep within, one that never lets me know for sure what it is up to. That's the strange thing about something that's incurable, something that's inactive, or as the oncologists say, "indolent." I keep my head in the sand, and Connie keeps her eyes on the calendar while checking the daily look in my eyes to see if she can outguess its next move. There is one uncomfortable, continuing theme in this dilemma: every time I get a sniffle, a rash, a sore muscle, a cold, or begin feeling down we always wonder, *Is Wally knocking at our door?*

After a certain passage of time, I fantasized Wally into a nonexistent entity and began ignoring him entirely. Although my numbers had not entirely returned to normal, my mind and body adjusted to the remaining minor negative effects of the disease, and I found a new normal in living an everyday life.

The years passed by, and to be honest, I tend to forget the things I do not want to remember. I don't call it pretending; it's more shades of ignoring or nonacceptance. The reason I have been able to do this is that I know Connie will worry about it for me.

The ministry is sweet. We enjoy visiting and speaking at both the megachurches and the small places of worship in our fascinating land. When we share in ministry with some of the greatest pastors of our time, life does have a nice, easygoing flow to it. I love the people we meet, the places we travel, and I really like having a job I didn't choose, a calling that chose me.

I don't always feel as good as I would like because the life on the road can be rough. A daily diet of restaurant food is not that good for my health, plus the ever-changing strange beds, awkward time changes, and traveling tensions associated with air travel could be the reasons that lately I am getting more tired than usual. I am also getting older. I know now for sure, that I will never be nineteen again.

I just wish I felt better. It's hard to explain.

Chapter 14
TATTERED

Ken had been complaining of "just not feeling good" for some time. Because WM is incurable, we live with the constant, underlying fear of the day it may return—when, as we had been warned, "it would wake up and make its move." Even though Ken had responded miraculously well to the experimental chemical therapy well over a decade ago, we were both aware that we had gone long beyond the time boundaries of its expected effect.

So we found ourselves in a world where we were living somewhere between denial and fear because of that negative expectation. It began looking like symptoms had returned to the point that denial was soon replaced by the presence of fear. Ken became more and more withdrawn. We both dreaded going through this again, and I needed answers, so we decided to see if I could get an appointment with a well-respected doctor at Stanford who specialized in his rare cancer.

—Connie

t's interesting that when we lived by the ocean, I walked alone most of the time. It was as if there was a tight, personal relationship between God, the water, and me. No one else was invited to join us. After we moved to the mountains, Connie and I began walking together most of the time, so there are four of us—God, Connie, the mountains, and me. We have a different dialogue with God as we deal with what might be happening. There is a sense of familiarity; wondering about Wally became a constant theme for our conversations.

I find that I am not as invigorated by the pines and the earth smells that leach out of the mountainside trails as I was when treading the yielding sands with sea birds overhead and waves crashing at my side. It's all God's creation, so it's not as though one is better than the other. It's just that, for me, God is more real by the waters—or should I say more colorful, like the tint I use when painting the inside of my head with his promises. The mountains suggest an association to the more private side of my being. I have a tendency to retreat inside more in the mountains, whereas at the ocean I would speak out, reach out, and stretch out when exploring God's Word.

We have favorite trails and back roads that we like to walk on. There is one special trail I like to walk alone. Connie thinks it's scary because it's too remote and a tad too deep in the woods for her taste. The trail is rougher, rockier, and less defined, but these are the attributes that separate me from everything outside and make it easier for me to talk to my Father. I feel more alone there; and like things were at the ocean, that's when I feel closer to his creation. It was on that trail that I stopped in the middle of my walk one day. I saw a small clearing off to the right where a log and a shaft of sunlight drew me in. I entered as into a cathedral.

The trees joined my thoughts as they surrounded and enclosed me. I could not get away from it; I knew something was waiting just around life's bend, and there was a foreboding familiarity there that scared me. I didn't like what my gut was trying to say to me about how I felt. I usually don't think about stopping for a rest when I am out walking, but it seems I was finding excuses to do so more often. I sat on the log and began doing a combination of thinking and praying at the same time. I know it sounds corny, but I had been doing that so much that I started calling it "prinking"—maybe I was spending too much time alone with myself.

In times like that I feel like a lyric from the Rolling Stones song "Shattered": "Look at me, I'm in tatters!"[1]

Sometimes it's tough being a Christian when hardships strike. We're all human and that means that we're susceptible to pain, doubt, exhaustion, anger, frustration, fear, and the whole gamut of human emotions. These experiences come in a swarm when you face cancer. When you know and trust God, this can cause the journey to become an even bumpier road, especially when you have been dealt a cancer that dogs your steps as you try to move on with your life. That's when the experience of facing death turns into a confusing journey between faith and questioning—with no foreseeable rest stops.

This inner tension is about doubting a God whom I do not doubt. It's about having trouble believing what is going on when

I believe God knows what he is doing at all times. It is about questioning what is happening when I happen to know where all the questions are answered, and I agree with every Word of the book that has these answers, and yet . . .

Dr. David Jeremiah says it this way: "Cancer is like elevator music; it's always there but you don't have to listen to it." Like me, this pastor has been there in the most visceral way. And like him, I feel that there is always this empty melody playing in the background of my experience, and unfortunately I have danced to that tune before. So when I come to a rest in the now familiar score, I pick up my Bible and God refreshes me with his words and a new song, a psalm of promises and hope.

I also see lyrics from my past as I peer ahead: "We can work it out. Life is very short, and there's no time . . ."[2]

Chapter 15
PATHÉTIQUE

Ken was reluctant; he didn't want to return to dealing with Wally, but he finally acquiesced. I was able to get an appointment for March 23, 2009, at Stanford's oncology clinic. I can remember the oncologist looking him in the eyes during his exam, and asking, "Where do you hurt?" Ken couldn't explain it. WM is the kind of cancer that feels like it is everywhere in your body until one day it goes somewhere specific, and that is when things get ugly.

The oncologist decided to do a complete checkup by ordering a variety of new tests, along with full-body PET and CT scans. All the tests were completed by April 20, and nothing showed up. There is something discouraging about knowing something is wrong in your body but having doctors tell you they don't know what it is.

This feeling was a lot like the prelude to the eventual discovery of this cancer the first time. If Wally wasn't moving in again, then what was happening? We returned to that empty feeling that goes with wondering about what was going on.

Before, this back-of-the-mind tug made Ken seem . . . remote. The Stanford trip seemed to have made him more . . . distant. There is a difference.

—Connie

f life is a symphony, I felt as though I had become the overture to a very dark piece of music. A short drive from our home is a place called Natural Bridges. We parked our car and took a long, steep pathway down to the bottom of a deep canyon. Once there we were rewarded by the presence of a vibrant stream and a picturesque grotto. I felt like Tchaikovsky that day because I had gone to that verdant amphitheater to clear a rush of thoughts out of my head. These thoughts were like the opening notes of some unfinished composition, and I knew deep inside they were the prelude to a mysterious scenario about to unfold.

I have always been fascinated by the music of Peter Ilyich Tchaikovsky. He was known as music's great sensualist. He would complain that there was so much music in his head that he couldn't get it all out fast enough, to the point the pressure gave him severe headaches. I think he got the best of it out when he wrote his sixth and final symphony, known as *Pathétique*. I say this because if you listen deep enough, you get the sense that he showed us his heart. One cold winter he took that mass of melodies ringing inside his head into a river. He stood there, up to his chest in freezing water, and waited for the quiet to come. This picturesque endeavor failed. Ironically it wasn't this suicide attempt that ended his days—he finally died from drinking. He inadvertently drank a glass of polluted water at the height of a cholera epidemic, and it is said that he succumbed in great

agony. He did this nine days after his *symphony no. 6* received a tepid reception at its premier.

As is the case with favorite artists, musicians, and composers, our familiarity with their work and the fact that they repeat themselves is often what we like about them. That is the reason I love Tchaikovsky's music and why I sensed something familiar was happening in the way things appeared to be playing out in our lives. Were Connie and I returning to the familiarity of waiting rooms, needles, and test results? I admit that having those thoughts by a bubbling brook was a little incongruous.

My dilemma was not nearly as dramatic as Tchaikovsky's struggles, but let's just say that people who have spent their lives in the music and entertainment business tend to react to things a little differently than most. That is why I deal with things in a grotto and frame my searching in terms of classical masterpieces. I can identify with the maestro in the area of having so much going on in my head that it hurt, and I needed to get it out.

Entertaining the possibility of the onslaught of a major illness or another cancer battle was as much a mental ordeal as it was a body battle. My mind was so filled with thoughts about how things were, used to be, or were going to be, that when the intrusion of an unplanned and unwelcome visitor entered its limited space there was a lot of immediate confusion and juggling. Again, all previous thoughts about myself seemed to become deadened in that new scenario. There were no more complete thoughts, but instead everything seemed to get lost and submerged into the possibility of the return of an insidious disease. Something was happening, and it was something familiar, but if it wasn't Wally coming back, then what was it?

So I was standing there in that dark grotto with my even

darker thoughts when I adjusted my focus and looked out through the large opening into the daylight. I saw Connie sitting by the stream, eyes closed, her face lifted to the sun, and it was obvious she was praying. I asked myself, *Do I go deeper, or do I join her?* She was reaching out. I was caving in. I needed to get in tune with her. I walked out into the light and sat down beside her.

She was humming our wedding song, one of the Judds' first big hits: "Mama He's Crazy."

Chapter 16
PASSING UNDERSTANDING

A few months passed after our day in the grotto without much change, and then we went to Nashville the following June for some book promotion events and Ken's appearance at a special charity event with Phil Keaggy and Wynona Judd. It was supposed to be a full week of activities, but most of the things fell through, leaving Ken with an open schedule after the concert.

I had already driven to Kentucky to visit my folks as I always do when we go to Nashville, but this time I stayed a few days longer than usual because my mom was really going downhill in her health. That was when I discovered that she could do almost nothing for herself, even bathing. It's hard to have a feeling for what is actually happening with your folks with only weekly phone calls when you are twenty-five hundred miles away in California. When I drove back to Nashville, Ken mentioned to me that he was so very tired that he spent almost the whole week in bed. That is so not like him. I was surprised.

—Connie

had never slept so much. I spent five days in bed. I was not sick or hurting; it was just as if my whole body did not want to do anything but lie down and be still. It was actually a good thing that my appointments fell through because I don't think I would have accomplished much by attending.

I had been upgraded to a giant executive suite at the Hilton when we checked in, and I remember looking at my digs thinking what a waste all that great space was. The rental car sat idle in the parking lot while room service and visits to the lobby restaurant were my only activities for days. I lost my appetite for everything but food.

When I woke from long hours of sleeping, I would lie on my back staring at the ceiling, talking to God. What is interesting about that time is that I never really explored in my mind what was happening with me or tried to put a natural or spiritual spin on it. I had finally walked away from worrying about Wally because the tests had shown that he was not back at my door. I think my subconscious was working overtime, though, and that coupled with the strain of holding it down and keeping it in check was making me tired. I was wrestling with something vague. And, I think not being able to put a face on my foe was wearing me out.

I did begin questioning God about his "peace that passes all understanding" on the flight back from Nashville. I was not exactly challenging him, but I was—in a kindly and spiritual way—pointing out that he wasn't really delivering in what I considered a clear and timely manner.

I pointed out some fundamental facts just to help him remember how I was doing my part: (a) I believed every word he said was true, (b) everything in me trusted his holy Word, and (c) I firmly believed he kept every promise in his Word. I also believed as a fundamental truth that, blessings followed obedience, so I threw in the fact that I also prayed for the gift of obedience every day, in Jesus' name, as a blanket approach to my spiritual walk. The point is that I wanted to make sure I had all the bases covered. I not only claimed these truths as an "at-home belief system" but also faithfully presented them when traveling and speaking at churches and special events across the nation.

As my full-on spiritual, physical, and mental weakness persisted, fear found its way into my mind and I became more certain of what possibly lay ahead—and it wasn't good. I cornered God and put it straight to him: Why was I not experiencing any peace, the one that passes all understanding, if I was doing everything he was telling me to do? I did not *understand* why I was not at *peace* and (respectfully) requested an explanation before too much more time *passed*!

I am not sure what weight baseball bat he used, but when he hit me with the truth, it had the ring of a game-winning home run. He must think I listen better in a dazed condition. Before I could get up and dust myself off, he told me that I was looking at that promise as a premise *and* from the wrong angle. He began by lovingly explaining that I was interpreting it, "I need to understand so that I can have peace." He then gently inserted the knowing in my sorest inner being that the way it works is, "The peace comes when I don't lean on my personal understanding and analysis of a situation. The mechanics of the process is that his peace will permeate my very being when I pass all my stuff on to him and let him be in charge." As he put it, "It is not about understanding; it's not about knowing; it's not about clarity; it's about obedience and trust." You know, as in "trust and obey, there's no other way."[1]

The plane hit a patch of turbulence, and the physical shaking seemed to jostle my thoughts into a sensible order.

I got it. It's a peace that *passes* all understanding!

When we fly home from back East it is typically a fifteen-hour day from the time the hotel wakeup call comes to the time we open the door at our home in the Sierra Nevada mountains. We live more than a hundred miles from the Sacramento airport, and part of the drive is on mountain roads, so I was exhausted after a day of connections, delays, and driving. I had been tired for almost a week, and the trip from Nashville to California wiped me out. Connie put me to bed while she took care of putting things in order now that we were home. Once again, I slept for days.

I couldn't understand.

Chapter 17
THE SECOND TIME AROUND

Our next doctor's visit was later that same month with Ken's local oncologist to follow up on the Stanford exams that had come back clean, and the doctor casually mentioned to Ken that he should have his prostate checked because of a slightly raised PSA test result.

"Nothing to do with his cancer but something worth checking out."

I called to book an appointment and found out that our local primary doctor was leaving on vacation the next day, but his nurse worked us in. Living in a small town does have its advantages. I dropped Ken off at the doctor's office and ran my usual small-town errands—post office, market, a drive down Main Street—and then went back to pick him up.

—Connie

need to run some tests, so I'm sending you to the clinic in San Andreas. While you are there, I want them to take a look at something."

The office was not that inviting, but the man in the white coat was warm and gentle. He's exactly what you want. He has that Norman Rockwell, family-doctor feel. There was always a sense of calm and no hurry. The session started with a handshake, a brief discussion of the weather, and a review of local politics, which was always limited because there wasn't much going on politically in our small town—mainly just restaurants and galleries. It was a "guy thing" visit, and the doctor's mood was pretty laid back, though there are times when all the chattiness and familiarity feel a little disconcerting, especially when it flows over into the exam.

I realized that this was his workplace and he thought nothing of stopping in the middle of a procedure to talk. It's just that when he stopped in the middle of my exam, an exam where I was laying on a cold table, with my lower half open for business, the guy thing and a lengthy conversation felt a little uncomfortable. I never have felt like yakking it up when someone is putting on the familiar rubber glove, especially when I'm at a postural disadvantage. *Snap!*

Subtracting that discomfort, the minutes ticked by as usual, just as they do in a regular town on a regular day. Nothing irregular until . . .

"I need to run some tests, so I'm sending you to the clinic in San Andreas."

I was stunned.

The doctor rolled the glove off his hand, turned his back, and jotted down some notes. I got dressed. When he finished writing, he laid down his pen and without turning around he began rubbing the back of his neck as he looked up at the wall. Talking to an anatomy chart hanging there in front of him, he told me he had felt something in the exam, possibly a small tumor; he needed to have me checked for rectal cancer. He walked me to the reception desk and instructed his assistant to make an appointment for me with a surgeon at the hospital two towns away. There was an unusually abrupt ending to my visit, very atypical. He wouldn't look at me, but I detected a certain look on his face.

Connie and I live in a very small town. Because things are small and local, the relationships and caring tend to be big and personal. I'm more than a number at the top of a manila folder or a coded data entry on a computer when I go to my hometown doctor. I have a first name. He knows me from church. We pass in the aisles of the local grocery store. We pick up our mail from the same post office on the edge of town. We have a sense of each other.

I had a sense of him that day.

It was mid-June in the mountains—that time of year when the weather is both crisp and warm outside. For me, everything went foggy and surreal. A familiar awareness tucked inside that moment followed me through the waiting room and outside to our car where Connie was waiting. I had come to the little white house on Main Street that contained the offices of our only doctor for a routine matter—then out of nowhere came that unexpected twist. It was all unclear and undefined, but I knew that something had just happened, something far from routine.

When I walked out of the building I must have had a look on my face, because the minute Connie saw me, hers matched it. She was leaning against the front fender of the car reading e-mails on her iPhone when she looked up and noticed me coming her way. Before I could say a word, she knew—that sudden sinking realization. Down there in our guts and bones, we both knew that our lives had changed. Nothing was going to be the same from that moment on.

We just stood there face-to-face, a foot apart. No words were exchanged. There was a light breeze in the air. It carried all the thoughts on its own. Our arms were at our sides; without raising them, our hands touched and held. Twenty-five years of togetherness filled the empty moment with subtle nuance, a soul connection with almost too much information to sort and sift. So we stood and remained silent, just looking at each other, into each other.

Why did we have the feeling that we had been there before?

Chapter 18
GUTS BALL

When Ken walked out to the car on that gorgeous, sparkling June afternoon, the kind when you find yourself so thankful to live in such a place as our quaint village in the Sierras, I knew immediately that something was wrong by the look on his face. He told me that the doc had found something during his rectal exam and immediately set him up with a surgeon in a nearby town to do a biopsy.

—Connie

One doesn't have to be a genius or prophet to know that a dark cloud was blowing in on that beautiful summer day in the foothills. The earlier softness of the morning mountain air quickly dissipated into the beginning of a familiar harsh reality. What lay ahead was not going to be a warm, fuzzy, feel-good kind of story.

This may sound strange, but although there were no words spoken, there was a sense between us that we were peering deep into each other's souls. We were united in the knowledge that we were one in God's purpose. It was if we were exploring the depths of our oneness as we were wondering how this was going to affect us, not only as a couple but individually. A rush of emotions filled the moment, without a word being said and without a clue of what was going to happen next. The heaviness that crossed our hearts did not actually have to do with fear, paranoia, negativity, or bad attitude—it was more of a *knowing* thing, or should I say a *gnawing* thing. Our heads didn't know what was going on, but our guts got it.

It is from the darkest nadirs in our lives that we must be able to rise up. Without the bottoms, there could be no tops. I recognize this when I look back at the way I grew up, in a simple shack on the edge of the Nez Perce Indian reservation. It is because of those cold, hungry northern Idaho nights, huddled on straw mattresses waiting for the warmth that the morning sun brings to the new day, that I realize that I am so glad I had that beginning.

I know there is a strength deep down inside just waiting for those crucial times it will need to surface. Like most of us, I have had tough times, and though every ounce of my worldly might has been aimed at smoothing things out when the bumps come, I know I can always count on that part of me that will rise up out of the Idaho dirt, kick in, and stand firm for the onslaught. I understand how blessed I am that God brought into my life a special lady who has also suffered and survived some of life's hard-hitting tragedies. She knows where to stand at times like these—by my side and on his Word.

Whatever was going to happen next didn't matter; we just knew we were in it together. I also knew it was finally time for some words, not words to be spoken between us but words to be offered up about us. So as we were standing there, looking down at the ground, I began to pray silently:

God, I love the way you orchestrate our lives and set the order of things to come. We are hurting at this particular moment because we can't seem to get our world going our way—but deep down, where that other strength dwells, I know this is where you are just waiting to show us the glory side of your nature. Thank you, Lord, for what looked like lumps and bumps, I can now see as flexed muscle and grit.

I knew then that in facing what may lie ahead, it was not about the falling down but the getting up. I was once told that the muscles babies use to stand back up after they fall when they're learning to walk, are the same muscles they need to develop in order to walk. When God sends a trial my way and I feel that I am having a setback, I know if I just trust in him and his promises I will see that struggle is what I need to move forward. It gets me off a spot I am stuck on; and if I will not move from it then he will perfectly move me to a place from where I can advance to where he wants me. But I have to give myself over to him for it to work.

FATHER, IF THE SPOT I AM STANDING ON NOW IS not where you want me, please move me from my perceptions to where you want me to be in this situation. But Father, if this is where you have placed me for your good purpose, please hold me fast and do not let me move from this place until you have accomplished your purpose in this part of my journey.

I raised my head, opened my eyes, and looked over at Connie. She raised her head, opened her beautiful green eyes, and they found mine. I asked her if she had been praying and she said yes, but she added that she wasn't going to say amen—because she wasn't done yet.

I motioned to her to get into the car. I walked around and got in the driver's side. Staring straight ahead, I turned the key to start the motor. Without turning to face her, I placed my index finger to my lips, backed the car out of the parking lot, and headed toward home in the understood silence.

Chapter 19
DOG SPELLED BACKWARD

We could not get in to see the surgeon until early July, so we had to sit with a scary unknown for a couple of weeks. The two-week wait until the appointment felt so very long, but we both tried to live our lives "as normal" as possible. I'm not sure how much we talked about it, but I do know how much more precious my husband became to me. Life is so very fragile, and it is so hard to live in the moment. Ken wanted to stay quiet about it until we knew if it was bad news, then once again he wanted to only share it with a few close, trusted friends and prayer warriors. So, in this waiting time we decided to spend my birthday in Monterey/Carmel after Ken spoke at a church in that area. God is good, so we just enjoyed each other and the coastal beauty to which we both feel such an attachment.

One of the things that came to my mind on the way home from the coast was that God made the appointment with our local doctor available to discover this thing early because it had not shown up on a recent PET/CT scan or two prior rectal exams. And there were many times ahead during this trial that I had to remind myself that God had already intervened.

—Connie

B ecause I did grow up next to reservation lands in the Idaho panhandle, the American Indian culture became an underlying part of my makeup. I never thought anything about it until many years later when I realized how much wisdom had been imparted to me as a youth. One account in particular really spoke to me as I was considering what lay ahead.

One of the elders from the nearby Nez Perce reservation used to tell the story about an old member of the tribe who had become a Christian. His name was So-bo-ta, and a few months after his conversion he asked the pastor who had brought him to the Lord if he could meet with him. He told the pastor that he was having a hard time dealing with a personal struggle in his Christian walk and that he felt like there were two dogs fighting inside him. He said one dog's name was Faith and the other dog's name was Fear. He said these two dogs were constantly battling inside him, and it was driving him crazy. The pastor looked at him intently, thought for a minute, and asked, "Well, So-bo-ta, which dog is winning?" The old Indian squinted his eyes, stared off in space as if watching a movie, and then answered in words so soft that they were almost inaudible: "I guess the one I feed the most."

That's what had been happening with Connie and me as I faced the possibility of dealing with another cancer. I realized and admitted that I had been feeding the dog of fear and letting the dog of faith starve. I also realized I had been doing that for a long time.

After that realization, my walks in the mountains became much longer. Instead of looking out across vast distances of rolling water off the Bodega Bay harbor, I began looking inwardly as I walked among the trees and on the mountain trails that looked out over distant valleys. I was still me, he was still God, and at that point it was still a confusing dialogue as I bounced between fear and faith, but at that time it wasn't the dogs that were howling—it was my unbelief.

I confess that I have a habit of looking the other way when I sense something bad is coming my way. That trait in my personality probably has something to do with growing up in hard country and wanting things to be different than the way they were in my austere existence in northern Idaho. I have always clung to a philosophy that if a bad thing happens in my life and I freak out, then I have two bad things happening in my life. Therefore, if I do not worry about it, I have only one problem instead of two. My reasoning may be one lamb chop short of a mixed grill, but it works for me. I have it all worked out. Or do I?

As I pondered these things on a mountain trail I had never walked before, the light of the day was dimming down. I walked until I was tired. I talked to God until he was probably getting tired. I stopped in my tracks, leaned against a tree, and from the side of the mountain I stared southeast toward the snowcaps in the distance that revealed the northwest edges of Yosemite. I was pulled into its magnificence and then reminded of the One who created it and me. He knows my name, he knows my heart, and he knows how to take care of bigger things than my tiny fears and potential disasters. I realized how much time I had spent fearing what may lie ahead, and with a few simple words imparted to my soul, it took him just a moment to chase it away with the big dog of faith.

I used to walk up from the beach to our house in Bodega Bay after long sessions with my heavenly Father. Today I walked down from the mountain to our home in the Sierras. Up or down, in or out, faith or fear—at times like these I always have the same destination—home and Connie. I always know I can find God wherever she is.

Chapter 20
RABBI TRAIL

While we were waiting to see the surgeon, we were given a series of tests to do at local clinics. Mentally these preparations seemed to hammer home the fact that there was going to be a hard reality to face very soon. We drove home after the last one and sat out on our deck having our "patio time" with a glass of wine. Ken looked at me and said the words we had left unspoken to that point, "From this day our lives will never be the same again."

I was horrified to hear him say something like that—it not only made me very sad but also scared me out of my wits. Oh God! Why, why, why? I could not believe that Ken (and I) might have to go through another cancer. I knew Ken was frightened, too, and that was so hard to witness because he is always so strong in everything he has had to face or overcome. Everything became blurry for a while; I guess we both became a little numb.

—Connie

With the sensation of a second sailing into dark waters now lodged securely in our consciousness, Connie and I decided to drive down the mountain the following day to make our customary retreat to the ocean whenever things needed sorting out. After a three-and-a-half-hour drive, we arrived in Bodega Bay and parked the car above Salmon Creek Beach on the north end of town. There are certain times when we pray better alone, and over the years we have set aside favorite places on that beach to pray. This was one of those times. We picked our way down a steep path along the cliff to the beach, separated, and headed off in opposite directions.

I walked about a quarter mile, stopped in a familiar place, and looked out across a sea of promises. I had been there before, so I knew how to wait expectantly for his Word. I breathed in the prickly, moist salt air and felt encouraged because I knew this battle belonged to him. I sought solace in that vibrant setting and experienced familiar comfort as my eyes searched the horizon. My prayer deepened, and I discovered that the waves had washed away all remembrances of the battle that took place there with the first cancer. The beach had been washed clean before, and I had come to pray that it would be again. I sat on the sand, feeling his presence, wrapped in his mercy, and warmed by his grace. Contrapuntal reflections ebbed and flowed through my mind like discarded extra verses of songs past. I came to rest, the music stopped, the key changed, and although I was not sure I could remember the words, I remembered the tune. Like the tide before me, my faith came washing in and out in a steady rhythm.

Scripture hurts at times. It is so hard when I remember all the incredible promises about healing and comfort, and then find myself sitting on a beautiful beach wallowing in the throes of doubt and discouragement. During those episodes of skepticism, times that appear to have no other reason or logic, I forget everything I know about him. My mind, heart, soul, and spirit know his truth, and yet I have lapses and begin complaining. I knew I needed to watch my step, but off I went, stumbling on open ground!

I began grasping at straws, trying to reel in parables and promises so I could get back on track with what I knew in my heart, when an odd remembrance came to mind. The unique cadence and sound of an old rabbi's voice, who had spoken at a local church not far from where we lived, joined the moment. I remembered him telling us about a traditional Jewish belief that we are all tied to God by a rope, and when we leave his purpose for our lives through disobedience, doubt, fear, sin, or questioning, in essence we sever that rope. We cut ourselves adrift and subject ourselves to all kinds of dangers and traumas because we are not only outside his will but we place ourselves outside his circle of heavenly protection. Here's the part of his account I like the most because it shows what a good God we have.

As the story goes, when we realize the error of our ways and return to him in confession and repentance, he simply ties the rope back together—and look what happens in that process. The knot that ties us back to him uses up some of the rope, so that the rope is shorter and *we are even closer to him than before*!

These knots represent our trials, and the rabbi's message to us was that our successful handling of these situations in a godly manner and our returning to him in contrition will result in drawing us closer to him.

Once again God caught me off guard by giving me that little story, and I was blessed with a moment of peace. It is such a strange tug-of-war, this back-and-forth thing between my God and me. I am my own pitiful psalm. Like David I start out complaining and questioning God, and by the end of those little episodes my heart takes over and I end up praising and trusting him. He asks us to have childlike faith, so I must really be pleasing to him—because that's how I go about it. I pout, scream, and throw my little spiritual tantrums until I am sent to that room in my heart where he eventually comes in and tells me how much he loves me.

I felt something strange and thought I had wet my pants until I realized that I had been so engrossed in his presence that the tide had seeped up under the sand to where I was sitting. I stood up and walked away from my silent chat with my Father holding a damp, sandy towel around my waist. There were no real words exchanged that day, only a sense of the ebb and flow of his wisdom conveyed into my being.

I made my way back up the rocky trail to the place we parked the car. Connie was leaning against the front fender with the windows open, listening to her favorite Amy Grant song, "Out in the Open." She smiled at me curiously because I had a sheepish grin on my face and I was panting like an old dog from the walk up the steep trail back to the road. I opened the towel to show her my wet pants, and her smile widened into laughter. I jumped into the car. As I changed into dry clothes in the backseat, people walking by probably thought I was one of the surfers who daily visited the place. We needed to come here more often. God is so easy to find on the edge.

I looked down at my hands; they felt red and rough, almost as if they had rope burns. I love it when God gives us visual aids to go along with his stories.

All the way home we laughed and talked about our encounters with God by the sea that day. Because we left Bodega Bay late in the afternoon, it was very dark when we arrived at our home in the mountains. Nothing had changed, but when we walked inside, the house seemed empty. We augmented this spatial impression with our silence, hardly talking as we got ready for bed. I fell asleep immediately—so soundly that Connie said she checked me twice to see if I was dead.

The next day I checked in at the hospital where I was to see a surgeon. They told me I was scheduled for a biopsy. It's funny how clinically things are handled in clinics. I sensed a routine and sequence of events beginning to unfold that I disliked immensely. Sitting in the waiting room, expecting my name to be called at any moment, I kept thinking back on my abbreviated visit with my hometown doctor. It was just a regular day, and then everything came in a rush.

As I sat there the cloud of undefined impressions, feelings, and fears suddenly took a concrete and heavy shape. Those emotions were starting to become facts. I didn't have any more details yet—I was still just waiting, right? Deep down I understood why I was there. I was beginning another long journey. It was perhaps a bit strange that I knew that dark fact with such certainty, but sometimes the worst really does come true.

The new reality loomed so large that I could hardly recall the reason for seeing my doctor in the first place. But the reason actually didn't matter anymore. What I did remember was that look on my hometown doctor's face as I was buttoning up after his examination, the one I had never seen before, the sign of the new reality.

I know it's not this way with everyone, but typically for me, when I am sent for follow-up tests, my natural assumption is that everything will come back negative—which ironically is a positive thing. It usually does turn out okay, even in cases where things don't look good going in. That day was different though; there had been something in my doctor's voice—and in that look.

So there I was, sitting in a clinic, waiting for a surgeon who wanted to take a tiny part of my body so he could decide what to do with the rest of me. I had utter certainty about what was transpiring, but it only held for a moment. If I allowed that thought, the one that kept invading my mind the other day, the one about having been there before, I was afraid I would get scared.

While I pushed it off, the fog settled in again, even more densely. I traveled back in my mind to a similar feeling from the old days—my time in the entertainment industry. It was like one of those days when I would get so stoned that I couldn't move and nothing made sense. Those moments were like this one. I found myself sitting, staring, frozen in time, frozen to the chair, unable to move or to think. That seemed better than fear. I fought to hang on to the just-being-stoned sensation. At least that would wear off after a while and life would return to normal.

Except, I had been there before.

Chapter 21

THE LIGHTNING AT THE END OF THE TORNADO

The surgeon did the biopsy on July 6, and we got a phone call from our oncologist on July 8 as we were driving to Southern California to attend a Love Song reunion concert at Chuck Smith's Costa Mesa Calvary Chapel. The oncologist gave us the news that it was anal cancer, not rectal cancer as first suspected, and the tumor could not be removed by surgery. Ken would be doing chemo and radiation instead.

We had been hoping for good news, so this was a heavy bit of information to hear while driving on California Highway 99 South. But we were glad that we would be spending time with Christian friends and meeting Chuck Smith and his family for the first time. Ken was able to have close friends gather round and pray for him and love on him. Well, it was a beautiful, sweet concert, and the whole sanctuary was full of love, joy, and a sweet fragrance. It was so obviously a God-ordained evening that it was like a soothing and calming balm to both Ken and me, almost as if God wanted to touch us with something special during this transition time.

We sat on the front row, and I cried along with Pastor Chuck as he relived the beginning of the Jesus movement in that very room almost forty years ago. Love Song was the signature band for the youth revival, and this was the first time the original members had been reunited onstage. We were blessed with the holiness of the moment.

As we were hanging out in the green room afterward, Chuck's daughter told me I looked like Farrah Fawcett. It had to be the hair, because no one had ever told me that, but the irony of it was that Farrah had died two weeks earlier of the same cancer that Ken was just diagnosed with. The fact Ken and I had recently watched the grueling documentary film of Farrah's dying days was almost too much for me. It was spooky.

—Connie

F or anyone who has grown up on the prairies and wide-open spaces of our country, lightning is a physical reality and not just an interesting flashy phenomenon that you occasionally observe off in the distance.

As much as our worldliness likes the idea of us standing tall and above it all, that is not the best stance when it comes to fire bolts falling from the sky. If you are the highest point in an area when lightning decides to seek the ground, then it will, by nature's decree, go to the closest point to the sky. This means, if you are "standing tall" in an open field, that point will be the top of your head. If you hide under the biggest tree, then you have also placed yourself under the automatic strike zone when it decides to land. And don't buy the old myth. Lightning *can* strike the same place twice.

It was a good thing for me, as it came roaring down on me a second time, that I was standing in the same place when it landed. I was standing on solid ground in my faith in my heavenly Father. I believe that if we put our trust in the Lord and take a long look inside that we will be surprised at just how much there is to us. The deeper we look, the more we discover the depths of our belief, the degree of our strength, and how his light shines in the lowest points of our darkness when we call on him. Yes, we do wrestle with the devil in many areas, but that dirty demon is like a cockroach and flees when the light shines in.

Lightning does have this predictable yet at the same time quirky thing about it. It always strikes without warning, and we never know where it will hit. Even if I did get advance notice, I know exactly what I would not do. I would not move an inch from where my Father has placed me spiritually, because I know that as long as I am where he wants me to be, which is being faithful to his purpose, then that is all I need to know about my next move. I have a clear-cut plan of action. I will reach for my Bible, raise its life-giving power up past my heart, open it to its unchanging promises, and then hold its peace and protection above my head. It's all in there, and the holy of the holies will cover me. And yes, though I found myself walking through valleys with death shadows a second time, I knew his rod and his staff would always comfort me. In his perfect time, he would lead me out onto the meadows of his boundless love.

I love the words in my Bible, especially the ones underlined; especially the ones underlined two or three times; and the ones found on the most worn pages, the wrinkled ones that have tearstains and are highlighted with yellow marker.

I love the words of other scribes who have pored over these same pages from other times, other places—saints I may never meet until we are gathered together in God's waiting arms in eternity. When we share our words, we find out how we are so much alike, especially when we aspire to be like Jesus. Then as we expose our hearts, we get the exciting privilege of seeing how gracious our Savior is by making us so unique. This uniqueness comes to some believers packaged as a gift in the form of insight so that they can shed new light on various timeless teachings in God's holy Word. They breathe life into passages and parables that may have passed the rest of us by if we lived alone in the confines of our distinct individuality and understanding. It is through these shared offerings that we find we are holy—wholly his child. It is holiness we seek as our constant, our goal, our dream, our calling, and our destination.

As I considered the trials we go through and the astonishment we express when lightning does strike us twice or a tornado knocks us down three times in a row, it was hard not to ask, *what could this precious God I believe in have to do with something like that?*—especially when we were seeking his holiness. A good friend handed me the following thoughts from fellow author Douglas Wilson that put a poetic point to that dilemma and helped soften the blow of an impending doubt trip. In that writer's uniqueness, he sees things in a distinctively beautiful way. I know God gave him this revelation so he could lead others out of the storms that so often surround us. In Douglas's words,

> Holiness is wild. Holiness is three tornadoes in a row. Holiness is a series of black thunderheads coming in off the bay. Holiness is impolite. Holiness is the kind of darkness that makes a sinful man tremble. Holiness beckons us to that darkness, where we do not meet ghouls and ghosts, but rather the righteousness of God. Holiness is a consuming fire. Holiness melts the world. And when we fear and worship a God like this, what is the result? Gladness of heart.[1]

I am so glad that I am my Father's child, that he never leaves me and that he is always there watching over me, the apple of his eye. Gladness from misery may sound like some weird kind of perversion, but God said it in such a wonderful way when he told us he would give us "beauty for ashes."[2]

I can really hang my hat on that and can say with blessed assurance that it will take more than two lightning strikes and three tornadoes in a row to knock it off.

Chapter 22
WAITING

My mom had hip surgery on July 7, and I had hoped to fly home to Kentucky to be of help when she came home from the hospital, but now I could not go. I knew my place was with my husband, and I know my dad knew that too. But I believe he would have really liked having me there. It was beginning to appear that she was not doing so well with home healthcare, and she started having other health problems as she went in and out of intensive care following the surgery.

We met with a new oncologist on July 13, and things moved very quickly from there. Ken wanted to get this treatment started and over with as soon as possible and so was set to begin chemo and radiation on July 20 after going through another string of tests, a colonoscopy, CT scans, an MRI, lots of blood tests, chest X-rays, you name it. We spent a part of almost every day either in a hospital or doctor's office when we got back from Orange County.

—Connie

f you were to ask people who have gone through the ordeal of a serious illness, dealt with a chronic disease, or endured major surgery to make a list of the things that bothered them most about the process, they will likely be united in what they consider to be the number-one aggravation.

Needles are bad, orifice-probing exams are uncomfortable, hospital food is less than exotic, grumpy nurses are a special kind of pain, complications and drug reactions are just plain awful, but there is something much more irritating. It is the inner exam rooms and the waiting time spent there. Once there, patients are usually left in a state of undress and often forgotten in the sterile cube, often with something sticking out of their mouths or elsewhere. Sometimes, when the wait becomes unusually long and I fear that I have been forgotten, I begin having visions of everyone going home and leaving me there alone for the night.

I have often thought of sending doctors a bill for my time. I pay them a premium fee for theirs, and in my real life, other people pay me to come to certain places, at certain times, for certain lengths of time. If I am booked to appear at a clinic or a doctor's office, if I am going to pay them for their time, and if they want me to linger there for countless hours, then I feel I should be on the clock also. Of course, this useless fantasy expands into visions of revenge against the entire medical profession. The degree of the desire to someday get even is directly proportional to the length and discomfort of the inconvenience.

I honestly believe there has to be a better way of going about doctor visits and appointment times.

When the new cancer became a part of my life, I knew what to expect and accepted the fact that this was the world I would be living in for quite a while. I had better buckle up for the ride. Early on in putting up with that almost daily routine, I recall an 11:00 a.m. appointment that had been scheduled with a specialist at a clinic in Sonora.

There were about a dozen of us sitting in the waiting room. One by one, people were being called in to the inner rooms, and I wondered, as it was half past eleven, why I was still sitting there. I asked the person next to me what time her appointment was, and she said 11:00 a.m. The person directly across from us, half asleep in his chair, overheard the question and gave the same answer. I asked the question to the general population of the room and there were several additional 11:00 a.m. appointments waiting to see the doctor.

The reality of the situation was that for the doctor's and staff's convenience, it was easier for them to have everyone arrive at the same time so they would have no interruption in their scheduling—the sheep could just wait. It became very clear that our little group with 11:00 a.m. appointments did not, in the doctor's opinion, have any value assessed to our time. I was furious, and so were the others when we discovered the betrayal. You could almost smell mutiny in the air. There is something about sick, old people when they get mad that has a special vibrancy to it. Grumbling under the breath has a great dynamic when there is a bunch of people all doing it at the same time.

I think part of the reason that this insensitivity on the doctor's office's part was so unacceptable to all of us in the waiting room that day was because we knew what was going to happen after we were ushered into the examination rooms. That move only made us feel as if we were progressing, but the reality was that it was just another ploy to keep us from realizing how long it was going to take.

Lobby waiting rooms are not that homey to start with, but at least they are better than the cold, barren inner rooms, and that's what makes this next phase even more excruciating. After a waiting period that feels just short of forever, a patient is near exhaustion from doing nothing, but the final blow is yet to come. Although it may be the shortest in length, it is by far the cruelest. The doctor spends about three minutes with you, tells you he is not sure what is going on with you, and schedules you to come back for another follow-up appointment.

The above scenario is not a pleasant thing to start with, but for people who have to experience this several times when going through major trials, or for older people who live with constant visits to medical facilities, it has a way of building up into a major problem.

I am coming up on a happy ending here. One day I was waiting in a crowded waiting room, and as usual, appointments were running behind. The nurse came out and called the name of a nice looking elderly man; it was his turn to come into the inner offices for his appointment. Without getting up he looked her straight in the eye and said, "Heck no, I am not going in there to sit in a cold room with my butt hanging out of some gown while I wait for another hour until you guys are dang good and ready to see me! I am going to sit here where it is warmer with my clothes on and look out the window at the trees and breathe air without a dirty gauze smell until we are both ready to go about our business here." With that he turned away from her, waited for a few seconds, and then turned back to the stunned nurse. "Tell the doctor I will be ready when he is."

Cheering in a waiting room is not normal, but neither was this guy—he was a saint, a hero, someone to be admired and honored for honesty and bravery. It was an ABC Network News "Person of the Week" moment. It was an "I'm as mad as hell, and I am not going to take it anymore" moment. He spoke for us all, and everyone there left with the sense that a small victory had taken place in our dreary lives. I needed this encouragement as I prepared to begin a long series of treatments. I had a new mantra to carry me through.

"Tell the doctor I will be ready when he is."

Chapter 23
PRIDE AND LOST DIGNITY

A chemo PICC line was "installed" on July 20, and the ordeal began. It started with a five-hour chemo infusion. Everything was going as planned until Ken got a call on his iPhone from his good friend, Jack Oliver (former head of Apple Records in London) while in the chair in the infusion room. Jack now lives in Southern California, and in Jack's fashion, he opened the conversation with, "What . . . is going on? I just got this e-mail forwarded to me, also copied to masses of people, telling about your 'anal cancer.'"

Ken wanted to keep this quiet for a lot of reasons, one being that once he's been identified as one who has cancer, the first question out of folks' mouths after "hello, Ken" is almost always "how are you, really?" No one means any harm by that, but after a while, it gets old, and he was tired of being identified that way. I totally understand, but it's very hard for me to keep things to myself.

Unfortunately, in sharing this with only our closest trusted friends—one of them took it upon themselves to send it to someone who sent it out to media on an international basis. So, now the whole world knew, and that's not what we needed to hear right at that time. Talk about toxicity; angry emotions and feelings of betrayal rose up in both of us. I was livid. "How dare you mess with my husband?" I was ready to fight! What were we supposed to learn from that? God help us! That was the beginning of me feeling that my faith was being shattered.

—Connie

was stunned.

It was our plan to keep the news of my anal cancer a secret except for notifying a few of our closest friends and a handful of select pastors across the country who would pray for me. I didn't want our hometown circle of friends and the public to know because I had been down that road before. People treat you differently. You are forced to take on a new identity, a disease persona that becomes very uncomfortable. As is the case with most cancer patients, we do not identify with the cancer and its specific nomenclature and we feel miscast when our new role is given to us.

I remember when the news got out about my first cancer, people would come to me with furrowed brows, drooping countenances, and with saddened, funeral tinged tones in their voices and ask how I was doing. That was a good thing about them but a bad thing for me—they were caring and wanted to help when I was down, but it always made me feel uncomfortable. The repeated solicitations concerning my condition actually became unwelcome after a time.

I really did not enjoy talking about my rectum. I longed to be asked how my hapless Raiders were doing, where I went to church, or what I thought about the last *American Idol* episode instead of being asked to give a rundown on the ugliness of my disease. Another thing about good friends that became awkward for Connie and me were the generous outpourings of offers to help with chores and bring food. It got to a point where I would rather have gone hungry and have the lawn become overgrown instead of having people around when I felt lousy. However, they did come and did do these kind things, and we love them dearly for it.

I am reminded of the time I was in the hospital, full of tubes and meds, after I contracted adult chicken pox because of my compromised immune system from the first cancer. People wanted to come sit outside the isolation window of my room in the intensive care unit to keep me company. It was as if I was speckled crayfish in a neon fishbowl. I felt awful, looked worse, and simply wanted to lie there alone and get it over with.

My decision to keep the second bout a relative secret was based on the wisdom Saddleback pastor Rick Warren embraced when his wife Kay had to face the beast. Rick knew if he went public that his thirty-five-thousand-member congregation and worldwide following would totally overwhelm the quiet and strength they needed to see it through.

Of special interest during the time of my second cancer is the fact that Pastor Skip Heitzig (pastor of Calvary Chapel Albuquerque, Beatles fan, friend, and leader of the Beatles-based Christian group, The Good Shepherd's Lively Hearts Club Band) and his wife Lenya found out on the same day that she had a major cancer challenge. While I put the public awareness lid on mine by going underground, he put the word out, pulling in every supporter and prayer warrior he could enlist to join him and Lenya in taking on the creature. He blitzed the Internet, Facebook, Twitter, and more, opening the door wide, enlisting a giant army of God's faithful as a way to defeat the enemy. So there we were, friends, with identical beliefs in God's loving purpose in our lives, taking two entirely different approaches. There was no wrong or right in our decisions—just the manner in which we preferred to press into our Father and his resources.

Connie and I had planned to share my diagnosis with only a few people close to us, our battle team. I decided to base my battle strategy on the story about Gideon and how he won his war with a small army. I do have to admit, though, out of pride, that broadcasting to the world that I had anal cancer was not the lasting picture of me I wanted to have lodged in people's minds in case it was my last hurrah. We prepared a brief and vague description of my malady for the outside world because I did have to give a proper reason for suddenly canceling speaking engagements that were coming up during the treatment and recovery period. In the process I contacted one of my close friends who is a Christian brother and with whom I shared the graphic details of my situation, so that he could contact a promoter to cancel one of the dates, a Beatles event in Nashville. (My friend had been the original go-between in setting up this particular appearance.) Because this event wasn't booked by my agency and because I didn't know the promoter personally, I asked him to take care of it for me.

It was a secular event, one of the few I had agreed to participate in over the years. For some reason, the organizer of the event would not take the simple explanation that was offered by my friend, that I was very sick, needed extended treatment, and would be unable to appear as planned. My friend finally backed down under pressure from the promoter who insisted on a more complete reason. To be expedient he made the mistake of copying the e-mail I had sent to him with all the gory details of my where-the-sun-don't-shine tumor just to get the fellow off his back. Because this promoter had international associations involved concerning the event, he took it upon himself to forward an exact copy of my private and rather descriptive e-mail to his mailing list around the world. This was particularly upsetting because all he needed to do was say I had to cancel due to illness or personal reasons. Anal cancer was not a necessary ingredient in his explanation. Because he was so into the Beatles thing, I think he felt he had an exclusive and enjoyed being the first to let everyone know about my illness—especially the nature of it.

I was completely unaware that this exchange had just transpired. There I was, naively sitting in the infusion room at the hospital beginning my first treatment, thinking it was going to be a private thing, a tightly held secret, a cautious plan, intact and cleverly in place. I was having a hard time and was a bit out of sorts from just going through the awful experience of having a port (PICC line) installed in my upper body so they could keep a continuous flow of the toxic drip going into my veins twenty-four hours a day (more than two hundred hours worth before the chemo portion would be complete).

I did not like the strange world I was entering. I am into visual aesthetics, and it was not Tuscany I was looking at through the window. Various bags were hanging overhead restricting my view, tubes were connected to the newly implanted contraption, and just a few minutes earlier the little levers had been turned on to let the juice flow into my body. I could feel the fluid invasion almost immediately.

It may be psychological, but I sensed something like a chemical, metallic sewage concoction running madly up and down my whole body, making its U-turns in my mouth and toes. I became immediately lost in what I was entering into, and experiencing what was entering into me, when my cell phone rang. I didn't want to answer, but I could see that it was one of my oldest friends from the Beatles/Apple days, Jack Oliver calling.

Jack was one of the few people I was going to share this personal news with—it was obvious that I was a little tardy in letting him know, and I was embarrassed that I hadn't treated our long-standing friendship with more care by letting him know right away. During previous trials, Jack was always the one who let me know he cares—I mean, there he was with his crusty, hard-edged Englishman persona, yet he was the only one who always sent flowers and budding plants whenever I was in the hospital.

His opening line was something like, "What . . . is going on, man? I thought we were friends! I mean this is over forty years later, and we have gone through some stuff together, and I have to hear from London that you have cancer in your butt?"

(As an aside, my including Jack in the small group of friends was not asking him to join a prayer circle. We decided a long time ago that there was a basic difference in our belief systems, but we have a proven friendship and a history that holds us together—plus we genuinely like each other.)

I admit it was probably all in my head, but I was not handling the first infusion very well, and it was uncomfortable. As I had only told a few people, I asked him how he found out.

As Jack explained it, rather crisply I might add: "Well Ken, it seems a clear description of your anal cancer went from you to a friend in Nashville, who then forwarded your private e-mail on to the promoter of the Beatles event you were supposed to attend. This @*#%#^! twit"—Jack's eloquent description of the promoter verbatim—"then forwarded it *intact* to the international Beatles community, promoters, publishers, writers, fan clubs, and wordwide media including a reporter for the Nashville *Tennessean*, your old hometown newspaper, by the way."

Author Tony Bramwell, ex-Apple executive and part of the old UK Beatles gang, was on this extended list, and they immediately called Jack in LA from a café in London, asking him what was going on with me. Unfortunately, Jack was clueless and a bit miffed. He hung up the phone and immediately called me on my cell. He feigned anger at me, but he could not hide the concern in his voice. This caring helped him accept my lame excuse for not letting him know sooner.

The content of his call dominated the opening day of a long ordeal. Hearing about the unwanted international scope of my anal cancer made me feel even more ill. When Jack explained how he found out, feelings of betrayal joined an already dire situation, took over and drove the moment into a deeper hell. The anger I experienced surprised me and seemed to be the overture to the darkness I was about to live in during the months ahead. It was the opening scene to the ordeal and the first of a few times when I would lose it. We finished up at the hospital, and I headed home feeling like a zombie.

A couple of days later I receive a nice plant at home from Jack and immediately named it after him. Jack the plant had a good life at our house, was well fed and always kept up to date on how I was doing. It had a prime observational position on the coffee table next to the couch during the worst of the ordeal. It was a good thing no one ever walked in while I was talking to Jack the plant when Connie would leave to run errands. I always used a slight English accent so Jack the plant would feel at home.

Fortunately, we live in a rather isolated area in the mountains, and the local community turned out to be the only people who didn't know what I was going through. Our local pastor and a couple of trusted prayer warriors from the church were practically the only visitors during the months of my imprisonment. Long-distance callers were discouraged from visiting because of the inconvenience of getting to our home.

So much for my dignity in this matter; my pride was going to have to wait for a better day.

Jack the plant eventually died. Jack the friend and I live on.

Chapter 24
GIDEON

They sent us home with a chemo pump that would infuse Ken every few seconds, twenty-four hours a day, for five full days. This would be repeated again during the treatment period. It sounded to me like a snake hissing, especially in the wee hours of the night. I prayed that the healing balm of Gilead would replace the chemicals flowing throughout Ken's body and that God would cause everything within Ken's being to line up according to his Word!

The next day would be the beginning of a grueling schedule of driving almost two hours round-trip through winding mountain roads to the hospital for a fifteen-minute appointment. We were to do this five days a week, for eight weeks of radiation. The thought of it was almost overwhelming. Knowing that Ken would be getting sicker and weaker with each day of having his body brutally abused by the combination of the chemo, radiation, and bouncing car would make it hard to make that trip.

—Connie

prayed for a scripture to hang on to during that time, but instead of a specific scripture God gave me a single word: *retreat.*

I was confused at first, and then I realized that once again he was talking about Gideon. He was talking about my tumor. With a small army, Gideon marched around the enemy with torches and trumpets as his weapons and sent them running.[1] I knew then that I was to break the jars of my disbelief and release the light of Jesus against the enemy. The trumpets of my small army were going to shout the prayers that would send this dreaded enemy into retreat, withdrawal, shrinking, and shriveling.

I had been attacked, and it was personal. I believed God's Word told me to fear not for he was with me,[2] so, instead of being fearful and accepting the position of being on the defensive, I decided I would go on the offense. The devil had picked on the wrong person this time, and when this was over he would think twice before he hit me below the belt again. A low blow to a child of the King of kings would not go unnoticed. I promised: *Like Nehemiah, we will rise and build. We will build with one hand, and we will fight off enemies with the other. We will not give in to hindrances or distractions, or to the ways of man. There will be many who will attempt to hinder us. We will operate by the power of the Holy Spirit and not by the mind of man.*

The daily two-hour round-trips to the hospital over mountain roads progressed from inconvenient to excruciating. Sitting in the front seat became unbearable in a very short time, so I tried lying across the backseat of our SUV. The problem was that I kept rolling off onto the floor every time Connie would slow down or stop suddenly. I tried positioning myself in the back by moving the passenger seat all the way forward, putting towels down to pad the floor, then getting on my knees with my chest on the backseat and my head on a pillow. The idea was to keep all the pressure off my tail—but sudden stops and sharp curves made this impractical also, as well as the fact that the hour or so each way in this position became extremely uncomfortable.

The final solution, which was bad at best, was to tilt the passenger seat back, put pillows on the two sides of the seat, and wedge my bottom at a forty-five-degree angle between them. Then I would place a pillow against the window for my head. Every turn, bump, and change in speed, even with this construction, was very uncomfortable. We thought of borrowing an old hearse so I could lie down, but then that would have probably freaked onlookers out—especially because it would be leaving the house more than once.

Arrival at the hospital was the jumping-off point for the next series of physical trauma. Getting out of the car without scraping the ravaged areas on something was impossible, especially when I didn't have the strength to hold myself up. Once out and standing up, the transition from the car to the treatment rooms became a four-legged adventure, with Connie's two legs carrying about 85 percent of the weight and creating most of the momentum. Hobble and groan, hobble and groan, making our way ever so slowly.

I made a deal with God from the very onset of the second cancer. I promised him that even though I may question him,

I would never bail on my belief no matter how rough it got. I meant it; I would stick to it, even though the whole ordeal might go beyond anything I would ever expect. I know that some people who have been through the same cancer may scoff at my descriptions and may even say they didn't have it so bad, but I also know that there are others who will accuse me of underplaying the horror of the experience. So the battle was raging, and I was in the very middle of the war zone. The pain was searing, and I was wiped out mentally, physically, spiritually, geographically, completely, and positively. I made my promise, and although my belief in him and his Word would not change one iota, I was aware that I was flesh. Although I had promised I would never question him or ask why it was happening, I did wonder why it was so horrible.

Here is the down-and-dirty crux of what goes on when someone believes this deeply. If I cried out and questioned him because the pain had gotten to the point of being unbearable, where did that put me? Was I denying him? Think about it: Jesus never considered denying God, but he sweated blood when facing the cross. Can you imagine how it would have felt for me if I had decided that I did not believe in his promises anymore because the trial I was going through was unbearable? How about the trial Jesus went through?

There was no turning back and nowhere else to go. The agony would be over someday, but eternity lasts forever. Faith is a fountain, and denial is a dry hole. I pled that I would be given the strength to hang in there because of my faith, and my reward would be that he would reveal the reason for the cancer. I ran my view on this by a close pastor friend and received some good and godly council. He told me I might never know the reason.

He said that God doesn't have to explain his every move to me. He also told me that if I was such an incredible believer then I should quit trying to make deals with God. "This is not a negotiation we are going through down here," he told me. He said he was sure God would let me know someday, but it might be on the other side.

Let me summarize: I asked for a battle plan, and God gave me Gideon. I decided to make a vow, knowing what Scripture says about the consequences in doing so. I told God I would trust him no matter what happened. I also asked for another deep, meaningful scripture to hang my hat on to help carry me through the ordeal. Something like, "Send me to the Word and blow me away with a real biggie that I can discuss with my pastor friends after the victory." You know what he gave me? "Be still, and know that I am God."[3] *Wait a minute,* I thought—*that's a Bible 101 verse.* I wanted something meaty, something earth-shattering. Then I stopped and thought how blessed I was to have received the perfect wisdom to hang on to.

I was to chill. I was to be still. I knew who was in charge. I knew who would see me through.

Chapter 25
IF YOU DON'T KNOW ME BY NOW

Our friends Scott and Nedra Ross wanted to know the exact time the trip for radiation would be made each day, so that they could specifically pray for us. That just blew me away; they knew how to pray for people, and they wanted to take on a specific aspect of the trial we were going through. Not the usual general prayer of healing but a prayer aimed specifically at the discomfort of the rough drive in the car on the mountain roads.

And it truly helped, knowing they were standing in the gap for us in that very specific way and time, and that God was answering their prayers, keeping us safe, and enabling us to actually do it. There were times when Ken would be in so much pain and so weak that I would almost become frantic wondering how in the world I was going to get him downstairs into the car.

—Connie

n the beginning, the radiation sessions seemed like nothing. I would get undressed, put on a thin little hospital gown and then lie down on a cold table for a few minutes. The machinery moved around the lower part of my body shooting at the prime target area from four different angles, and then I was sent packing. There was no sensation of anything happening, and it didn't appear that this was going to be the hard part. It was the chemo pumping into my body twenty-four hours a day that I feared and hated from the first time. I have always said that the artful purpose of chemotherapy is to kill everything in your body and then wait to see who survives—you or the cancer! I figured the concurrent radiation was used to burn up all the evidence in case the chemo didn't kill me.

I admit I had become a little cocky about how I was handling the treatment the first week or so. The chemo was what I expected, so I was prepared. I was taking enough antinausea drugs to keep the army's entire Third Infantry Division from throwing up after eating bad mackerel. I had heard of people having an easy time of it, and I knew I would be able to do my macho thing when it was all over by telling everyone how I breezed through it. Chemo was not a walk in the park, but it was the radiation that eventually took me to the edge—a clinging-to-the-brink experience of brutal pain and degradation.

Eight and a half weeks of daily sessions on the rack—in my mind no longer a table—turned ugly about halfway through. At first, I would come in, climb up, and position my body to their specifications. The radiation experience began with an initial session where they defined the tumor location and then tattooed my body with guiding marks that lined up with the machinery for the subsequent sessions. They also made a cast impression of the lower portion of my legs and my feet so that my body would always be in the same alignment each time I got on the slab— still can't call it a table.

More than once, when I was lying on the plank having heavy radiation, the sound system in the hospital would play either a song that was uplifting or an oldie that brought back fond memories. It was as if God was bringing songs of optimism to me in the middle of my hard time. The first time this happened was when the reality of what was going on had set in, and I was so weak from the combination of the chemo and radiation that Connie had to hold me up to make it from the car to the daily nuclear dose. That particular day was a turning point, and because music had been in some odd way my life's narcotic, a good song at the right time did soothe the pain. Once I undressed and put on my open-derriere gown, a nurse helped me into the atomic room and the young attendants lifted me up on the rack. I was so weak that they had to move my legs apart for me, and put them in the position they needed to hit their target from the various angles. I was gone. I was as down and as far out as I thought I could go.

I found out later that there were three of us "older men" who had started this treatment regime during approximately the same period. Anal cancer is a life-and-death situation, and I don't believe any of us realized the potential downside of the treatment. There are no alternatives; surgery is not an option because anal cancer is inoperable—unless you agree to let them remove everything from your lower body except your butt dimples. To me that is not surgery. I call it shock and awe. So your choices are few: hardcore treatment, demoralizing surgery, or eventual painful death. These are choices that are not exactly like deciding whether you are going to order the daily special or the lamb chops with mint sauce. I knew I was having a rough time, but I was shocked to later hear that the other two eventually opted out, preferring to suffer the consequences than continue with the horrors of the treatment.

As I lay there, I felt terrible, disoriented, barely clinging to an already sagging belief. I had become weary of crying out to God, begging for relief, and then wondering why he wasn't answering. It was challenging my faith because I had been hanging in there with him and giving him my all during the trial. The prayers for lessened pain went unanswered. The pleas for healing of the oozing burns between my legs and buttocks were ignored, and the physical damage was worsening. The lifelessness and hope-lessness pervading my mind was not being attended to; God was obviously ignoring me.

Those were my thoughts as I awaited the sounds that I now know were ravaging the norms of my south-central body. It was then that an old favorite song, "If You Don't Know Me by Now," began playing over the crackling sound system in the ceiling. "If you don't know me by now, you will never, never, never, know me."[1] I had no idea that God was a part of the Philadelphia soul music group Harold Melvin and the Blue Notes. The words of the classic oldie poured out of the speakers the way his words sometimes leap from the pages of the Bible.

The lyrics lifted me up and away from that table and sat me at his table. I was fed a needed meal and nourished beyond comparison by his Holy Spirit—the part of him that is always at my side.

From table to table. I was awakened from this reverie by a young intern shaking my arm—trying to get my attention—probably wondering if I was asleep, dead, or so wiped out that I had become unresponsive. He removed the cast, lifted me from the table, and helped get me to the dressing room. I couldn't move because I was so drained and weak that it took what felt like an hour for me to get out of the gown and into my clothes.

Even though I was physically devastated, my spirits were elevated by the song God had sent my way to carry me through the moment. Holding on to the walls for support, I made my way slowly to the lobby where Connie was waiting. She met me at the door and led me to the car. She stopped at the passenger door and before opening it, turned to look at me. I was smiling for the first time in days.

"What's that tune you're humming?"

Chapter 26

THE I OF THE STORM

I remember driving down the mountain to get mail and fresh greens for juicing at the local organic farmers' market and watching the owner while she went out to her garden and picked fresh kale, chard, spinach, green apples, and tomatoes just for me. It was hard seeing how everyone was going on with their lives as we were frozen in time on our mountain, trapped inside during a triple-digit August summer, raging wildfires visible from our deck. It felt as if we were being smoked in because of the fires outside and being burned out because of the cancer battle inside.

I felt invisible and numb and lifeless. Don't they see me as they merrily walk up and down our cute main street, stopping in for wine tastings at the local wine boutiques and having lunch at sidewalk café tables, drinking coffee, laughing, living? I always cruised Main on my way back up to our reality, and felt almost as if I were floating down the street without sound in the middle of a movie set, out of place, out of time, out of hope. Surreal, really.

Thank God, I had someone I could vent to and be brutally honest with about my feelings and my weaknesses, and that someone was Nancy Alcorn. Nancy is the founder and president of Mercy Ministries International, with scores of hurting souls to care for. But from the beginning, she called almost daily from wherever she was on the planet to see how "our boy" was doing. And she made it clear that I could call, e-mail, or text her anytime with whatever.

She never, never judged me when I would fall apart from the anxiety and the double trauma of having both my mother and my husband facing uncertain futures. I'm not sure I could have made it without her.

—Connie

Peace does not mean to be in a place where there is no
noise, trouble, or hard work. It means to be in the midst
of those things and still be calm in your heart.

felt like Elijah. I was lying at the mouth of my pity cave, and the earthquake, tumultuous winds, and fire of the cancer were raging about me. As usual, I was waiting for God to speak to me through the cacophony of the storm. It was admittedly bad weather I was experiencing, but because I knew God was holding his umbrella over my head, and because I believed he was right there with me in the midst of all that was going on, I knew my payoff for believing in him would come any day. I knew it was on its way. It didn't matter what violent elements were raging inside and outside my body; at those moments God is always closest to me, so "any day now" was when I expected to hear from him.

Darn that "a day is as a thousand years" deal!

That particular day, the cancer storm was not the only thing that was raging. I was freaking out with doubt and holding on for dear life to my promise to never bail out on him and to trust in him no matter what happened. Suddenly, I was knocked to the ground by the rocking realization that I was the one who was in the earthquake, the fire, and the wind—not God! I was the one making all the noise with my pleadings, demands, and crying out. I also began to grasp the sad fact that the truth was, I was not alone in the noise. That was where the devil lived: in the spectacular, the big events, and the raucous stuff that hits us up alongside the head when we aren't looking—when we take our eyes off the Father. The devil is in the earthquake, and he rattles us because it seems bigger than us. He is in the wind that howls so loud that we can't hear ourselves pray. He is in the fire that burns the pillars of our belief beyond recognition.

Because I was so physically and mentally weakened by the cancer and chemicals, it was not until I mustered up the spiritual strength to crawl out of that noxious insanity that I was able to completely understand that God wasn't in all that noise, and never was in it! Unlike me, he knew better than to hang out with the devil. It wasn't until I wised up, ran away from the inferno, and came to rest by a gentle stream that flowed from his Word that I began to hear that still, soft, sweet voice that quiets the storm, calms the wind, and puts out the raging fire. That was when I began to communicate with him. His Holy Spirit patiently waited for an opening and overcame me in my moment of weakness. And when I am at my weakest, he is my strength.

He is my strength by pushing all evil away from me when I am too weak to push through the attacks and winds that blow against me.

He is my strength when I am too weak to pull my own weight because he takes on my burden and pulls the load for me.

He is my strength when I am too weak to pick things

up; he picks up the pieces of my scattered dreams and makes them come true according to his purpose.

He is my strength when I fall down because it is by his power and force that I am lifted up and placed on solid ground.

He is my strength when I become irritated about my inability to overcome my trials by reminding me that he overcame everything that ever has been or ever will be in one simple act on a cross.

He is my strength when I get weary and can't continue on because he reassures me that with him I can go the distance; he will carry me through the brief journey here on earth and into the long part of our existence—eternity with him.

He is my strength when I face the horror of cancer because he reminds me that cancer is the little *c* and Christ is the big *C*, and that he is by my side the whole time. His good purpose will prevail, and that is all I need to know.

So, as my praise cranked up, the noise quieted down. My words of love for him melted into his love for me. I came to the calm in the eye of the storm, and that was where we met. It was peaceful, and I could hear his voice—words that had been pouring forth in tender love all the time. Never-changing words of love and hope, direction and care, words that hold fast in their content and intent. Everything settled down, and I was able to separate what was going on in my flesh and what was happening in my heart.

It was so simple when he explained it all in the hush. Sometimes it is just so hard to be simple.

Chapter 27
SCHOOL OF HEART KNOCKS

I would usually rise earlier than normal in the mornings during this time, and that was my precious, quiet, peaceful time with my Father. He heard everything. I was turned inside out, raw and vulnerable, scared out of my wits and shouting and claiming every promise I could get my hands on.

I spoke these promises over Ken while he was almost always in a lying-down state. I can remember bending over him and looking him in the eyes and speaking these words of healing over him whether I felt them or not. I was desperate.

—Connie

When a couple as close as Connie and me were notified that I had cancer, a new personal dynamic entered our relationship. It felt as though we had been enrolled in night school to learn a scary new subject. It was a tough course to pass not only because of the homework; preparing for the final test turned out to be the hardest part. The way we used and occupied our home and the order of importance and time spent in different rooms changed drastically. Our car would be traveling new routes to less familiar places. Shopping became much less entertaining. Frivolous buying ventures disappeared as time and dollars were reallocated.

Patient and caregiver replaced the usual definition of husband and wife, and we were pulled into a new focus that was oddly foreign to the center of an existence that we were used to. Pride went out the window, and life got very real inside walls that became prisonlike because of the amount of time we were forced to spend there. The hours on the clock became meaningless as old routines disappeared and the disease became the taskmaster that dictated activities and timelines. Connie suddenly had to carry the full load while I grappled with my inabilities. Our relationship was altered by this unwelcome circumstance while our love deepened because of the situation.

In my case, life became simple in spite of being excruciating in so many ways: car, hospital, bedroom, and bathroom, kneeling before the porcelain throne. I called it doing the "rainbow yawn."

Reading hurt after a while, and TV bounced between friend and enemy. It helped pass the time, but I could only take so much of its blather. It eventually turned on me and became torture. Commercials eventually went far beyond being a nuisance to becoming an outright torment. Breakfast, lunch, and dinner were an enigma, as nothing sounded good and everything tasted worse. Kindness from friends turned into intrusion. Encouragement became almost hurtful, and prayers morphed into platitudes. The Bible alternated between comfort and aggravation.

Minutes felt like hours, and days appeared to slip by unnoticed. I writhed in pain for hours, and then discovered the deepest pain came when I heard my beloved in the other room crying in despair and empathy. The disease invaded all the corners of our lives—finances, joy, activities, plans, relationships, careers, worship, and in some ways the worst of the bunch—our identity. Loneliness surrounded the journey because we were collectively alone in the struggle. No matter how much people tried to help, the facedown-in-the pillow reality was that we had to ride it out by ourselves. Like a swarm of locusts, it ate away everything, leaving nothing behind.

The only thing that could have been considered more painful than the treatment and consequent body condition was what happened to my mind. The chemicals altered the pieces in my brain like a faulty Rubik's Cube. Chaos found a home in my head and moved into the penthouse. My mind was so blasted by the regimen that the struggle to gather all the pieces together in a simple, neat pile became like trying to play "pat a cake" with a nervous octopus.

In time, the trial became so encompassing that it became the only thing. It dissolved everything about me into one solid piece. Thank God that he was there with us during that time, skimming the dross off the top, waiting for the day he could see his reflection in us.

The inability to take in or contain nourishment eventually took its toll, and the great boredom of not being able to move about became debilitating. I missed my daily walk and talk with my loving heavenly Father. I would go off into dreams of the days when I would stroll by the sea or pray aloud beneath the mountain pines. I wanted to feel him in my face when we talked, as I had in those days. I was getting so I couldn't confess on the couch anymore. I needed the awesome, overwhelming example of his magnificent presence in the crisp morning air, in the alone places where no one could intrude on our oneness.

In those settings my total nothingness became abundantly clear. The dream deepened and became a lesson in his love. And looking back on it, I realize how blessed I was to be able to visit his world. There I was surrounded with the magnificence and richness of his being. Because I belong to him, I share in his riches. I am an heir to his kingdom. I am a child of the King, and royal blood surges through my veins. It covers and cleanses me now and for all time.

I walk with the King of kings during moments spent in the magnificence of his creation. I enter the holy of holies and dwell in the presence of royalty. I am wrapped in the warmth of his sovereignty, eternally blessed, sheltered by mercy, and loved unconditionally. I am a child of *the* King, and I stand before him in his courtyard each day. I praise him for the beauty that surrounds me and for the splendor that fills every part of me in the form of his Holy Spirit.

I prayed aloud skyward as words I did not understand

poured forth from my lips—lips privileged to say his name. I became lost in his wonder each time I remembered that I had been graciously found by his love, saved by his grace.

I was suddenly stirred from my reverie by Connie's entrance into the room. She was holding a glass of water in one hand and some pills in the other. I realized it was that time. I went from meditation to medication. My fantasy walk was over, but my walk in faith continued with God in my heart and her by my side.

Chapter 28

TAKE THIS JOB AND LOVE IT!

So many times during the eight weeks of nonstop trips back and forth over the mountain and through the woods to the chemo/radiation ward, I wasn't sure we would be able to do it again the next day, but we did. I can remember leaning against the windows in the hospital foyer, crying my eyes out after getting off the phone with my dad, after getting updates about my mom's fragile condition. I could tell he was scared and hurting, and to hear his voice crack just sent me up the wall. Why, God? I'm so torn—I want to see my mama and daddy, but I would never leave Ken during a time like this. It was interesting that my dad and I were experiencing some of the same emotions—he even said the same thing I felt—"I feel like climbing the walls!"

—Connie

lived my first few years as a new Christian scouring the book of Job, in part to see if I was a direct descendant. Connie couldn't believe what I was going through as she watched my life unfold, or should I say continue to fall apart at such a dazzling pace that if I was a horse, they would have put me down.

It is hard to imagine a hole deeper than the one I dug for myself during my decades of decadence. The big shocker for me was that as soon as I accepted the Lord as my Savior, things really headed south. She witnessed the sores festering on my tender spirit, observed the savage destruction of my family and possessions, and cringed as she watched the betrayals set in. As far as she was concerned, I was indeed a modern-day version of this Old Testament saint. The main difference between Job and me was that I knew I had brought my calamities upon myself. In street terms, I deserved it. I am confident, though, that old Job and I both felt blindsided by the unexpected downturn in our lives.

My two cancers came about a decade apart, but the minute I found myself immersed in the second battle, I began feeling that my life was a continuum of one bad ordeal after another. Job's losses appear to have progressed in a tight sequence, but regardless of his timely flow and my longer gaps between misfortunes, I know it was hard for us to keep smiling through it all. However, the part that was cool about Job and me was that both of us refused to defy or deny our heavenly Father no matter how down and dirty it became.

I pondered those things during the sleepless nights in my continuous quest to put the fragments together. It was part spiritual wrestling, part mental exercise, and part trying to not look down and see the results of the invasion to my groin. I'd lay with my legs apart in an effort to let the radiation burns breathe at night after each day's kamikaze attack. (Job's boils?) Dignity was no longer on the table. Surviving with my spiritual walk, heart, and crotch intact was the order of the day—and night, and morning, and afternoon . . .

I think I found more comfort in our differences (Job's and mine) than I did in consoling myself with the flattering thought of our similarities, or in identifying myself with such an incredible man. First, my fortunes had already been diminished by my past transgressions, so instead of losing a lot, I was trying to hold on to what I had left while being knocked out of commission by the treatment for seven months. Second, the friends who gathered around me never questioned my faith or the reason for the trial. We stood side by side in our approach to the situation; and instead of intellectualizing my afflictions, we held hands in prayer and supplication to God's holy Word. My friends did not bring accusations and condemnation, but, yes, they brought hearty food into our home and lawnmowers to our yard. Third, and most important, my wife never asked me to curse God and die, but rather to trust God and live.

I was like Job in that I hung on hard to my faith, an unfaltering belief that I had a merciful and good God who loves me beyond anything I could imagine. I don't have a clear picture of just how much Job's mind wandered before he came to the written conclusions we read about in the end of his story. I also don't know if deep down Job entertained the possibility of what his friends suggested—that he was suffering because of the consequence of sin. I know that I thought about those things a lot until I finally stopped listening to the devil's lies and jumped off that sorry train at the next station. Once I left the condemnation baggage behind, God sat me down and talked with me as he had with Job. He took me through a brush-up course on the wonders and paradoxes of his realm.

The one thing I do know is that Job and I ended up in the same place spiritually. (I wish it could also have been financially.) I know it was a rough go for both of us, one that seemed to last forever. The trials stunk worse than wet camels in August. I also know that we both came out the other end—faith intact and resting in the knowledge that our God is an awesome God.

Those were the kinds of thoughts that would invade many of my midnight wonderings, but this is how my soul and those nights would end: dichotomously rich! I was cursed with a disease but blessed by grace. I was writhing in current pain but remembering when I wallowed in past blessings. I was worldly poor and spiritually enriched. I was alone in my specific suffering while abundantly soothed by the embrace of godly friends and a loving wife. I was experiencing the good, bad, and the ugly. That's how this whole thing works. Romans 8:28 says, "And we know that all that happens to us is working for our good if we love God and are fitting into his plans." I could write all day and not come close to passing on an encouraging thought that offers more comfort than that. God *is* good—*all* the time! He *will* turn to good what Satan meant for evil.

The cancer nights were hard and long, and an oft-used plan of attack was to get my mind as far away from what was going on in my body as I could. Praying and going for God stuff was like leaving the planet and finding a safe place that offered diversion and comfort. Many times, in the midst of these spiritual soft spots, the renegade cells would make a counterattack on the invading chemicals launched to search and destroy, and I would be pulled out of the heavenlies and back into my reality. The cancer shrieked and tormented. I would check my bearings to see how far I was from the nearest bathroom and chart the shortest route. I had a plan. I was going to keep my eyes closed while doing the rainbow yawn on those nights so I could picture the devil's face in the still, porcelain waters before me.

Chapter 29
HEART OF THE MATTER

I felt that God gave me a couple of things to cling to from the start. One was a vision of him turning the chemicals being infused into Ken's body into his healing balm of Gilead. The other was this verse: "The earnest (heartfelt, continued) prayer of a righteous man makes tremendous power available [dynamic in its working]."[1]

Over the treatment weeks, Ken became so ill, weak, and skinny. He lost his hair, of course. I remember when he decided to have me take him to a little barbershop downtown to get a buzz cut so the fallout would not get in his eyes and mouth. That was actually one of our only outings during the whole ordeal. We were basically homebound or Sonora bound, where the hospital was located. As the burns got worse and pain worsened, I would hear Ken screaming out in torture and asking God to lessen the pain, but God remained silent.

I have heard other people also say that God seemed silent in the midst of their trials. But we both knew he was still with us—he was just being still. I really do feel that my faith was shattered and became shaky at times. The whole treatment was so clinical, brutal, and archaic. Why don't they consider the whole person? There's nothing about good nutrition or supplements, only nuclear bombardment with drugs, drugs, and more drugs.

—Connie

t was early evening when the darkness of the disease seemed
to escalate in its terror. The pain increased, the depression
deepened, and the battle between belief and disbelief inten-
sified. I pled for his hand to reach down and take it all away,
but nothing changed except my discomfort. It was at that point
that I painfully got on my knees and began offering up my usual
complaint to God. "How is it that you demand a relationship
with me, but it seems like you are never there when I seek you?" I
thought a relationship consisted of an exchange: I talk, he listens;
I ask, he answers; I pray, he responds; I seek, he fulfills; we chat,
we share; he guides, I obey; I sin, he speaks to me; he forgives
and corrects me, we are Father and son. This is my description
of a relationship—two people exchanging things!

In the approaching dusk, everything seemed the same. I was
pressing in, reaching out, and as usual he was being silent, not
there for me once again.

Then he answered in the stillness:

WE HAVE A RELATIONSHIP IN THE PUREST FORM!
You pray, and I do answer your prayers. I bless you
when you don't deserve it. I punish you when you don't
understand. You cry out to me with your problems, and you
feel I let you down. You hurt me and disappoint me. You get
angry with me, and then I fill you with my love. We are close;
we are apart. I question you, and you doubt me. We cling to

and love each other to the point of tears. Don't tell me, my child, that we don't have a relationship. We are family in the real sense; we are blood of the blood, and we are bound in an eternal covenant.

Like any other child who didn't choose his father, you didn't choose me. I chose you! You may try to leave me as a runaway leaves home, but you can never be separated from me. I am in you, of you, for you, with you; and because you know my Son, you know me, and we are one. You are my child, the apple of my eye. I knew you, created you, delivered you, and have ordained forever with you.

We have the relationship that the poets can only try to write about! I have given you a book of this love and suggest you stop murmuring in your tent and read it—then come before me and tell me we have no relationship! I have made you promises that no man can keep! Read my book and search your heart. Be still, and all your senses will feel our relationship as it embraces you completely and for all time.

I awakened from a room that, before he spoke these words, felt like a prison confining me to that ordeal. I found myself in the calm of a passing storm. I stared into the softened darkness in disbelief of the immensity of what had just been imparted to my spirit. I was lost and found. I was cold, yet my heart was warm. I cried out, and joy flowed in. I laughed, and tears filled my eyes. I swirled on the inner edges of a spiritual whirlwind; his power surrounded me, then I spun out into my helplessness and fell on my knees begging for his unending mercy, his unfailing grace, his unconditional love. He remembered his promises and forgot my sin.

We talked for a moment about eternity, and the hours flew by until I found myself wrapped in the glory of his loving arms. With great effort, I got up off my knees and stumbled back to bed, eyes down, and hope up. The night winds beat against the side of the house, and his heart beat inside my chest. I realized that he is the heart of all that matters!

Once again I was reminded that it's all about forgiveness—forgiveness!

Chapter 30
STAGE FRIGHT

I spent most of my time trying to come up with meals and prepare healthy foods that would appeal to Ken, and also juicing fruits and vegetables. Thankfully, there were a couple of organic farms close by and there was a bounty of fresh greens for juicing and fruit that was sumptuous. Peaches are Ken's favorite and were in season for a while, so he had tons of peach smoothies with protein powder. That and sharp cheddar cheese with grapes were some of the few things he could handle.

There was a huge forest fire close by that caused the hundred-degree summer heat to be almost unbearable. We always loved having our doors open, especially for sleeping, but could not because of the smoke. We were closed in spiritually and physically.

I was chained to the car, to Ken, long-distance phone calls to Kentucky, and the hospital for months. Part of our mental and physical health has always been our long mountain walks in the morning, but those were out too. Sometimes, in the afternoon, I would walk out to an open vista not far from our house where I had found a bench under an oak tree. I had never noticed this bench before, but I sat down and put my right hand out and asked Jesus to hold it and hold me. It was a respite that I looked forward to, and there I would once again hand Ken over to him and beg his healing for my husband.

—Connie

There is something incredibly lonely about cancer. Its emptiness, depth, stark reality, and immense proportions are overwhelming at times. My former perceived invincibility had become quickly diminished in direct relationship to my observation of its attack on my body and my being. Its viciousness was unmatched, and the power that surged forth out of the heart of its evil existence was brutal. The passage of time and the distance of purpose had cast me into an uncertain place, a million memories away from the cities, concerts, crowds, and careening choruses that filled and fueled my heart and hopes for more than a third of a century.

The applause had grown still with age, and the fading stars no longer came out at night, leaving me to face the unwelcome intrusion into my ordered world reluctantly subdued and at odds with almost everything I knew. Because I was going through a cancer trial for a second time, and because I was at that disturbing point in its sequence of not knowing whether I was going to make it, I became insecure. I gave in to my fears, expecting the proverbial fat lady to come running into my bedroom singing loudly, while clutching a torn backstage pass to her abundant and heaving chest. The show was over; it was a tragic ending that even Shakespeare would applaud.

But before the final curtain in this little self-centered drama came crashing down on the third act, God's very essence took center stage. The Maestro himself stood before me, and I offered my confession before his elegance in a cleansing moment of repentance and humility.

I always feel like a pretender when I come before the throne. Yet, he knows my heart; he cleansed and mended the filthy rags that I had wrapped around my soul. During this time I stood before him considering the perfection of his Majesty. Because he is perfect, there are certain things I could depend on, things that would never change or go away. Because of the godly things I deemed crucially important, he caused me to reconsider the earthly things, so I became more forgiving of the things that displeased me. I began to drift and eventually considered it all of no account except for the God I worship, the woman I love, and the children who are blood of my blood. I succumbed to the inevitability of this mysterious, perpetual exchange. Without realizing it, I had left the couch and was surprised to find myself standing at the window, staring through dampened panes into the leaves of a blossoming dogwood tree. I looked down, and worn slippers were touching my soles. I looked up, and his Word was touching my soul. I was completely unaware of what was going on inside my body. His presence overtook my being, and I knelt as I became filled with love. I forgot my lines. I became lost in him.

I could feel God on the cold, hard floor and delighted in that moment as his Holy Spirit filled me. His way is one of unquestioning acceptance. He asks so little and gives so much. He gives the most and gives it first. When I am able to look past myself and get a glimpse of his greatness, I cannot help but sense that I have fallen into his uplifting grace and stumbled skyward into the deepest and greatest relationship on earth.

If only for a minute, as I passed before his gaze he could

look down from above and say, "This is my child, in whom I am well pleased."

Oh! That would be a day of celebration—my happiest day of all. The very thought of being pleasing to Almighty God!

As I faced the situation, I felt the warmth of his loving hands on my shoulders. I listened quietly as he spoke silent words of blessed assurance into my waiting heart.

I was surprised by the strength I had been given to move from the couch and actually kneel in prayer. The effects of the chemotherapy, the radiation, the invasive tests, and the concurrent drugs typically left me helpless and languishing, a captive of my bed; but even then, kneeling in prayer to God remained a part of my life. In my weakest moments and sometimes with great effort, taking all I had within me, I would turn over on my side, pull my knees up toward my chest, reach my hands above my head, and close my eyes to pray. I would kneel on my side when I couldn't get to the floor.

This was my theater, my one-man show. I was not afraid for the curtain to come down. There would be an encore.

Chapter 31

DAYS OF YORE—DAZE OF YOUR

God made our way smooth with the help of our faraway praying friends and a couple of close friends, including our local pastor, Paula, who would bring food and prayer and kept herself available to us 24-7. We did not know then, but she had recently discovered that cancer had returned to her body after seven years of being healed without any medical treatment—only trust, prayer, and nutrition. One day when our car broke down, she rushed to the hospital to drive Ken home. Her constant and consistent peace and trust were so comforting to us. Oh, to have that kind of faith! When we found out later that she was facing a potential terminal cancer battle of her own and was spending her time ministering to us, without letting us know, we were so blessed with seeing what the word Christlike looks like.

—Connie

mmersed in the throes of chemical and genuine depression one night, I was struggling to be biblical. In an attempt to pull myself out of the painful morass, I tried counting my blessings.

That is usually a great idea, an almost fail-safe way for Christians to go when dealing with our worldly trials. Counting our blessings, combined with faith, usually works. I jumped right into the routine, but as I attempted to prayerfully recall the bounties of my obedience, my mind began drifting away from sacred things, and eventually the whole exercise turned into a flight of desperation. My little spiritual exercise of obedience quickly digressed into me just running from the pain. I soon found myself reflecting back on the old worldly days when I was indestructible. Looking back on those events made me realize that the only scripture that I could actually append to what I was doing was maybe the one about a dog returning to his vomit.[1] I am not saying these are bad memories; quite to the contrary. It's just that I often have this tendency to go back to the past instead of dealing with the ever-present *now* of a situation.

I am not sure which medication was the tour guide for this trip, but along the way I found myself back on the Apple roof for a while, and then I traveled from London across the Atlantic and the US, back to a long-ago California meadow and a special occasion. We were all so young, healthy, and on top of the world. We thought we had it all; in fact, we thought it was all ours. Those were the good old days, and because we were in a Hollywood state of mind, it was a good old haze we were living in. I guess you could say we were existing in a "daze of your"—your estate, your Mercedes, your hit record, your summer home, your agent, your manager, your accountant, your attorney, your production company, and your regular table at the Brown Derby.

We used the word *your* as if we owned these people and events—a word stamp on the collection of worldly stuff we had accumulated as proof of our greatness. I find irony in the fact that I now realize I was also on the slave end of this little ritual. As a producer, it was only natural that when "my" artists spoke of me, that I was "their" producer, or I was "their" manager, or I ran "their record company." Funny, I never thought of it that way before. It would appear now that the few brain cells the drugs didn't zap in the sixties and seventies have been mostly cleaned out by the chemo. The upside of this is that the remaining active ones are not so cluttered. I like to think that chemical cerebral housecleaning has granted me the gift of becoming less intellectual and, in some obtuse way, able to see things more clearly.

At the time, we thought we were all so cool—us, the beautiful people. It was so magical being in the middle of the in-crowd. When things eventually turned south for much of our gang, and as we one by one abandoned our dedication to one another, the reflections in our mirrors turned sour.

The heady hours of the past migrated into a dark future of severed ties. We came into our glory unprepared, and a reverse expectancy took hold because we had no idea how good it was going to get. Then, when we got used to it, we demanded more of the same in larger quantities, and we required much more fanfare and attention in the process. Because we stumbled into our menagerie of associates and associations, there was no sensible basis for picking logical comrades—we just happened, and we lived off the surfaces of our self-perceptions. We began believing our own press releases; skin-deep was as deep as it got, and boy was that fun. As shallow as that was, I think there is a good lesson to be learned from it all. When those of us who came out alive on the other side look back on those days—on that daze—we do have a different perspective.

Time passed in decade-sized lumps. We eventually settled down and sorted ourselves out, and once old wounds healed and unwanted memories faded, we became beautiful to one another once more.

More than thirty-five years later, after I left Apple and the center of the Beatles world, I accepted for the first time an invitation to appear at a series of BeatleFests. I could not believe that it was 2008 and seven thousand people were showing up at these annual conventions with their Beatles wigs, outfits, and tie-dyed shirts. I found myself submerged in old hippies hanging out in the lobbies of hotels singing Beatles songs and carrying bags filled with newly purchased Beatles gear and souvenirs. They would religiously attend our conferences and workshops, scraping our mental bottoms for any tidbit previously unturned or even wanting to hear the same old stories told once again by those of us who were there.

My initial reaction to these fans was on par with William Shatner's advice to the Trekkies: "get a life people!" But after three cities on this tour, I realized they did have lives, jobs, kids, and grandkids. It just so happened that they had a fun hobby, and they really had a good time every year reassembling with old friends, singing their favorite songs, and reliving those precious memories when the Beatles filled out the soundtracks of their lives—youthful innocence engulfed in elderly nostalgia.

Then something special happened for those of us who were brought in to share our stories at those conventions. There we were: myself, Pattie Boyd (Harrison), Donovan, Spencer Davis, Billy Joe Kramer, Nancy Lee Andrews, plus a few others from the "inside" coming together after almost four decades and getting to know each other in a new light.

In the old days we were all so crazy that no one knew where we were mentally during any given moment. Now we were a bunch of older people, sitting around enjoying meaningful conversations and telling war stories about those days. It was amazing how memories resurfaced and came alive once the retelling started. Half of the time it was wall-to-wall laughter when we shared our individual versions of the craziness of past events. There were the embarrassing drug and alcohol stories and the exhilarating reliving of wild rock concerts. We remembered things for each other and maybe embellished our roles a bit here and there.

The other half of our dialogue was more somber, even poignant, and often very touching as we looked into faded eyes, missing hair, and limited movement, remembering us as we were and missing those who were with us no longer. We edged along the contours of mortality, fearful and quiet, trying to both accept it and ignore it at the same time. Still, we enjoyed one another tremendously and went away glad we came, perhaps hoping that reliving the past would extend the present and take the teeth out of the future.

I indulged in these recollections as if they were painkillers. My mind escape took on the colors of an international tour—a

Magical Misery Tour I guess I could say—as I tried to distance myself from the current grief for as long as I could.

So I continued drifting, back to the innocence and unfettered days of yore when we lived in our "daze of your." Dealing with the contrast between that youthful virility and the reality of getting older, barely being able to move about from the effects of a wicked ailment, was my best defense for drifting back in time.

JANUARY 30, 1969, A
ROOFTOP IN LONDON

In my memory, I looked out across the downtown London skyline at the four Beatles playing in the freezing cold on January 30, 1969. We were there because we needed live footage for the *Let It Be* film. We had failed to come up with a location for a live performance in time to meet filming deadlines, so even though it was the heart of winter, we went on location by simply climbing a few stairs up to our own roof. Because we had locked the street-front doors leading into the building, all security could be handled simply by one Apple employee standing just inside the door in case of an emergency. Little did we know then that this would be one of the most historical moments in rock and roll, and that those of us who were there would be members of a very special and intimate society, eternally bound together by the sheer emotional immensity of that day. No one knew that would be the last time that the Fab Four would play live.

So there I was, in my sickbed, in my mind's eye, back on top of a five-story building in London's downtown business district.

I noticed in my return visit that two of them, John and George, were gone. I remembered sitting by the chimney stack with Maureen Starkey, Ringo's wife, and that she was gone. Ron Kass, Neil Aspinal, Mal Evans, and Derek Taylor, who ran things for the Beatles and were the innermost of the inner circle back then, were all there that day, and they were gone. Billy Preston, "the fifth Beatle," who sat quietly behind the band at his keyboards that day, was also gone. There was enough energy and enough exciting people on that freezing roof that day to light London nights for months. Now those of us who are left have a hard time getting the coffeepot running in the mornings.

That moment, that cold afternoon, that magical place has bonded those of us who remain, in a timeless forever. We keep in touch and care about our eventuality—there were only a handful of us and it was an extraordinary occasion. We didn't talk about it afterward; we honestly didn't know what had just taken place. We left the roof, filed down the stairs, and went about our business knowing that we had experienced something very special. We would sort it out later when we could understand what we felt that day. So we keep in touch knowing we are next, dodging the inevitable, and escaping the obvious. We have only in recent years begun putting those events in order. Our recollections have softened, and I believe we can see more clearly now.

MAY 2, 1973, A MEADOW IN THE MALIBU MOUNTAINS

George Harrison took the afternoon off from the studio to drive a considerable distance from Hollywood to the remote

seven-thousand-acre ranch in the Malibu mountains where I
was living. I was hosting a giant bash celebrating the launching of my new corporation, Hometown Productions, Inc. It
was a beautiful spring day, the sun streaming through the trees
as it cast long, soft shadows onto the meadow, bouncing off a
sparkling stream running though a wide canyon basin. Free-
range horses played in its shallows.

It was more than a launching of a new company. It was the
launch of my flight away from the big conglomerate recording
companies and my advancing desire to be free from all creative
constraints. This seed of nonconformity was planted and nur-
tured by my year-old relationship with Waylon Jennings and his
outlaw gang of musicians. Being around this Billy-the-Kid-with-
a-Fender-Telecaster persona resulted in my desire to break all
molds, musical and otherwise, and jump boot heels first into the
rebel-cowboy-madness world he owned.

I grew up country, and he sensed that commonality; we met
and something clicked. He and I immediately became musical
two-timers because we could not help ourselves—we wanted to
make records together. We were actually cheating on our legal
industry mates because I was president of a CBS record company owned by Andy Williams, and Waylon was signed to RCA's
Nashville division run by Chet Atkins. These formal relationships clearly stated that we were not to work together. Naturally,
this made our hooking up even more enticing. The forbidden,
melodic fruit we planted and harvested was exhilarating. His
West Texas rawness and my British rock-and-roll edge was an
alliance that could not be denied. Our outlook on our companies' restrictions and the outcome of his current and my new
outlaw attitude was this: I resigned from Barnaby CBS and he

put his band in their tour bus and drove out of Nashville, against RCA's will, to join me in my LA studio environs. Once there we made what turned out to be one of the biggest albums of both our careers.

So, this mellow, meadow day of severance, togetherness, and celebrating found Waylon and his wife and soon-to-be country recording star Jessi Colter joining people from both worlds. A gathering that included a who's who of family, employees, friends, hangers-on, aspiring musicians, actors, and a bizarre list of major stars of that era from the recording, film, TV, and artist community. Leonard Nimoy (Spock) was taking pictures of Patti Harrison and Waylon Jennings chatting. Rob Reiner (*All in the Family*) and his wife Penny Marshall (*Laverne and Shirley*) were chatting with Jack Oliver, president of Apple Records.

Jack's cohort at Apple, Beatles road manager Mal Evans, was spending a lot of time hanging around singer Claudine Longet. George and I were sitting on a log chatting about the late sixties when we set up Apple together, and discussing how interesting it was that he was currently running his own company, Dark Horse, and I was going independent with today's launching of my new corporation. Ricky Nelson and his artist wife Kris were sipping wine and listening to a classical horn quartet playing Eric Satie's sweet melodies under the trees, while farther away in the meadow singer songwriter Jennifer Warnes had joined in a mini hootenanny with *Hee Haw*'s Hager Twins and singer song-writer Ric Cunha. It was a strange brew of beautiful people who blended together on a California spring day during this amazing era and a vibrant time in my life.

I began feeling almost well in the recounting of these moments, until realities started creeping into the reverie. George died of cancer; Mal was killed in a hailstorm of police bullets; Jack Oliver had a serious, life-threatening bout with throat cancer; Rick Nelson died in a plane crash; Waylon died from about ten things, all of them ugly; and Claudine's whimsical world went down in flames in a shooting tragedy.

August 12, 2009, a crumpled couch in Calaveras County, California

Looking back on the daze of yore soon developed a different twist. We were on top of the world, mostly in our twenties and thirties, and compellingly unconquerable in mind, body, and spirit. There was nothing we couldn't do or have. We were smart, talented, and flush with cash. Excitement is what we had for breakfast, lunch, and dinner. I don't think any of us looked beyond the moment or place we were standing in, except for the awareness that another concert, event, or recording session was around the corner. I wonder what it would have been like if we could have stopped and watched a film of what the future held and how fragile it all was.

Like John Lennon, none of us saw what was coming, and as a leading presence in his band and the annals of rock and roll, he unwittingly became an early victim of a fate that began picking us off one by one.

I struggled to get up from the couch. Connie had left to run errands, so I used determination and focus on my mission to move from there to my office.

I pulled John's picture down from the wall, held it right up to my face, and peered into his eyes once again as if they would blink, a signal that he, too, was still wondering what had happened. I got down on my knees, took the glossy print out of its frame, and laid it down on the floor, so it and I would be in the same position we were in that day in my office when he left this world. Once again I had been left to wonder, and I felt very alone.

He said in his song "Tomorrow Never Knows" that we should listen to the color of our dreams when trying to figure out the vaporous bent of our mortality, that it was not about dying and that it was not about leaving. I guess I will always be a rock and roller, even when it comes to ethereal matters. It didn't matter what he meant or if either one of us understood what he meant. Those thoughts spoke to me because that's how we verbalized our feelings back then.

I asked myself, "Is this illness becoming my tomorrow?" Only God had that figured out, and I became confused as to whether I was accepting, doubting, or resigning myself to a mysterious inevitability.

It was in the midst of this quandary that I became aware I was on my knees. This made me realize that I had positioned myself halfway to the answers I needed. I had been struggling with that question under my own power for so long, so when I bowed my head, closed my eyes, and brought it before the throne, I was the rest of the way there—and I received an immediate response. God must have been busy that day because he was rather brief in his reply. That I should trust him, leave it with him, and his love would cover all was what I got for an answer. He told me to just take a look at myself—not exactly the personification of invulnerability, hey mate? He said he would get back to me later with more, now that I was finally getting it.

All my ramblings began blending together, and I realized that the meadow that day was just like the rooftop years before. Jack Oliver, Mal Evans, George Harrison, and I were there on both occasions, but both the meadow and the roof had some glaring similarities beyond the presence of the four of us. None of us who shared those experiences had any sense of the fact that we weren't going to live forever. We would have cancers, plane wrecks, assassinations, overdoses, debilitations, heart attacks, fatal gunshot wounds, amputations, and other unexpected endings to our forevers. Later years brought about unexpected failures, fallibilities, and disappointments in the way things changed course.

Using the Beatles as a base point in all this led me to discover that there are probably less than half of us alive today. George and John are gone, leaving Paul and Ringo behind. Waylon and Johnny are gone, leaving the other two Highwaymen, Kris and Willie, traveling alone. The Apple Corps are just like the picture on the record label—only half an apple. Derek Taylor, Mal Evans, Ron Kass, Maureen Starkey, and Linda McCartney have departed, leaving Jack Oliver, Tony Bramwell, Peter Brown, Peter Asher, and myself missing them. Ricky Nelson and many others who were there that day have left the meadow. My new company, which had assembled us together that day, died along with them.

The immortality of this reflection felt heavy on my heart as I lay like dead weight on the floor of my office, wondering where my position in these percentages would land in the few months ahead. John Lennon, Mal Evans, and Ricky Nelson met sudden fates. George Harrison, Waylon Jennings, and Ron Kass slid slowly down a dark slope into their stark and certain ends. It left me wondering where I was going to fit into this mix.

These are common thoughts when your mind and body are obliterated with disease, medications, and brutal treatments. I confess I would escape into those extreme past events that were laced with real narcotics, and then they would return to act as a narcotic of sorts in dealing with the pain of helplessness that overcame me in the darkness of the cancer battle I was engaged in.

If I were giving advice to someone going through the dark valley I went through, I would say go for it; go back to other times—remember the good. Trials are not fun, and I own that I sometimes leave my current spot on planet earth because I give in to my flesh and abandon what I know deep down. I sheepishly admit that this tendency to sail away from the current nightmare into old dreams and worldly ways of processing important matters is not a good thing or a godly thing. It's just me taking over the helm of a journey until I face the reality that the Lord is my captain, my wife is my shipmate, and the prayers of my Christian brothers and sisters are the crew that will guide me through this.

I finally gathered the energy to get up from the floor and made my way back to home base, the couch, leaving the picture on the floor. I dropped down onto the blankets and fluffy pillows Connie placed there for me. I nodded off, wondering if other people have sixties music playing in the background while they dream. I drifted back to the garden.

Chapter 32
BEAUTY AND THE BELIEF

Ken's last radiation treatment was on September 10, 2009. Coincidentally, his last treatment for WM had been on September 10, 2001. Unlike the first time, when the treatments ended, we didn't walk right away. Ken was physically a goner at that point. Our first outing was in November to Sacramento to join our friend Nancy Alcorn in taking part in the grand opening of their new Mercy Ministries home for girls. Nancy asked Ken to speak. He was still weak, but he gave it his all, as he always does. It was the perfect way to reenter society!

—Connie

Three months after the final radiation session, we received the news that the results of the first CT scan, blood work, physical exams were in, and it appeared the treatments had been successful and the tumor was gone.

It is a little strange to relate to what I am about to say or even imagine that someone would have such thoughts, but I actually miss the closeness I experienced with my heavenly Father when my pain was overwhelming. I miss crying out to him and pleading with him to bend down and touch me with his merciful and healing hands. I love hearing his blessed assurance when all seems lost. Nothing is more beautiful than sensing his arms around my being during these trying times. They let me know he is God and I am his. I am reassured that everything that happens is in accordance with his divine plan. Deep inside I know everything will be all right if I will just trust in him.

At times like these, he has a way of speaking to me through the absolute simplicity and clarity of his Word. In fact, it is so simple that his message needs only one word—*believe*!

He tells me that if I believe we must suffer at times without explanation, then I also have to believe him when he promises undeserved blessings. If I believe in humility and contrition, then I must also believe that he delights in giving us our hearts' desires. If I believe that I am to give the shirt from my back to my fellow man, then I must believe that I will drink fine wines from vineyards I did not plant. He did not give us his Word to select only the parts that work for us or condemn us. In addition, he does not suggest that we should go on a bummer bender and live out solely what we perceive as bad news. After all, he is the God of the good news! In fact, he asks us to see him not as a God of wrath but as a God of grace and blessing.

Either I believe or I don't—that has always been my mantra. I believe that he is perfect and makes no mistakes. I believe every word he says. I believe that it is not necessary for me to understand a lot or a little. Comprehension is not a requirement of my salvation. Faith is!

I love it in the Bible when Job repented after questioning God and cried, "I am nothing—how could I ever find the answers? I lay my hand upon my mouth in silence. I have said too much already."[1] How can I even think in my wildest dreams that I can understand his ways in my present state? He promises great revelation someday, and that is good enough for me. I am so happy he is in charge. It is amazing how much better I feel now that I have let go and let him take charge of my affairs.

The sounds of birds outside my window move me from these rambling thoughts about my loving heavenly Father. Their chorus validates my conclusions by its enthusiasm. The birds don't care if anyone else is observing, enjoying, or listening to their presentation. They are just doing what God has set them about to do. They only have one purpose—no questions asked—just forward, free, full-blown obedience to what they were intended to be. Oh how I long to fall in line with God's purpose for me with this same incredible exuberance.

I fall; he catches. I stagger; he straightens. I falter; he smooths the way. He is love; I am a partaker. I question; he answers. Because he is all, I need nothing. He is around me, in me, before me, and for me. Yes, I *am* blessed among men. There is incredible beauty in these moments. I bow my head; he lifts my spirit. I forget all the pain as he forgives, forgets, heals, and binds the wounds of my affliction.

He wept for me as he wept for Lazarus—out of compassion and love. He knows that more than any cancer, it is sin that can kill me. He defends me against worldly persecution as he did the adulterous woman facing the stones of hypocrisy. He grants me revelation as he did the woman before the waters of the well. He begs me to come down from the trees of my haughtiness as he did Zacchaeus so he can stay with me, sup with me, and draw me into his way and his purpose. He washes my feet with his humility and then teaches me how to walk. He turns the tables in the temples of my transgressions. He leads me to eternal peace, if I will just follow.

He is my Friend, my Teacher, my Healer, and my Savior. He is the beauty in my life. I am privileged to gaze into the eyes of this man of sorrows and hold on to his nail-scarred hands. He died for me, so I must—I absolutely must—live for him in return.

I recently read something written by Jan Dravecky in the NIV Encouragement Bible that really touched me. She entitled it "Brutally Honest":

> Brutally Honest . . . there's no right way to suffer. When I am talking to a mother whose child is dying of cancer, it does no good to say, "Don't feel sad" or "don't be angry at God." There is no point in saying, "You shouldn't feel that way." If she feels that way, she feels that way. Feelings are not right or wrong; but it is wrong to lie about how you feel. And you're no less of a Christian if you express those human emotions that come to the surface when you suffer. To me, you're more of a Christian because you are being honest.[2]

It will be five years from September 10, 2010, before they say the coast is clear—if the tumor hasn't returned by then. In the meantime, the first cancer is a ticking time bomb. To be brutally honest . . .

—Connie

AFTER WORDS

I open my Bible. Three years have passed, and Connie and I have just returned from the hospital. Once again we are told that the tumor has not reappeared. Each time we receive good news, it means we are getting closer to that wonderful five-year medical line in the sand that says I will be in the clear. We have two years to go, but this is encouraging, and we are definitely thankful.

I love my Bible, the one that Connie gave me more than twenty-seven years ago when I became a Christian—the one that smells like my shaving lotion. It is chock-full of underlined passages and different-colored lines from different years, but there are only a few scriptures that have a date beside them, out in the margins. I have only written dates at certain momentous points in my life, times when a special scripture jumps out at me, as if God had written it specifically for that moment and me.

My Bible falls open to Psalm 32. I have turned to Psalm 32

through 37 so many times my Bible assumes that is where I am going and automatically falls open there. I like to think of myself as a free spirit, but I am actually a creature of habit in certain matters, and it is to these worn pages I go when I get that special feeling that God is sitting beside me and is touching me with his hand in blessed assurance. It's as if he is saying, "Let's spend some personal time together, just you and me—let's bask in the warmth of our close friendship for a little while."

Other times I turn to him when I feel the need to crawl into his lap and put my arms around his neck, to hug and hold him— we all get lonely at times. Mainly I turn to these special psalms when I need to put my spiritual house in order. I have come here today for none of these reasons. I feel like I am between seasons. There is something wintery about the cancer struggle. I feel as though Connie and I are coming out of a dark jungle into a new day. It has been a long time in the trenches for us, and at this moment there is a feeling of hope in our lives.

What is so ironic about today is that I intended to read Psalm 32. To me, this psalm is a man's psalm—more specifically, a psalm that celebrates victory, the joy of being forgiven, and the blessed feelings that follow. (Not to say that this powerful psalm doesn't speak to women as well.) However, what jumps out at me is on the preceding page. In the margin of Psalm 31:14–15, two dates are written: 12/96 and 6/09. I remember writing 12/96 the day I was diagnosed with cancer the first time. I had also written down 6/09 next to that date—the month I found out about the second cancer. I clearly remember the day I wrote down that second date. God told me on that day that this was not new territory for us. I was filled with fear, but he reminded me that he had carried me safely through these mountains before. The message was clear—*here we go again*—but as always, he was with me. It is the only place in my Bible where there are two dates next to a scripture. I also notice I have written June 2009 in very big handwriting, and then I remember why. I did that so there would be no room for a third date!

> But I was trusting you, O Lord. I said,
> "You alone are my God;
> my times are in your hands."

God brings trials not to hurt us but to bless us. When I would ignore this truth and have those questioning dialogues with him, I would feel guilty. I was afraid I was falling short of what he required of me as his child. But I know now it was all good, that we were just chatting. Let me leave you with this: I *was* falling short the whole time. Every time I cried out and got mad because he didn't answer, every time I felt alone because I thought he had abandoned me, every time I believed he let me down by not answering my prayers, every time I accused him of breaking his promises, and every time I thought about giving up on him because of these things, I fell short. Falling short, he revealed to me, is what it was all about. Before, I used to stumble on open ground and fall all the way down. Now I fall short because his loving arms, tender mercies, and unconditional love always catch me before I hit the ground.

I close my eyes and lose all sense of where I am in this moment, but I am aware that I dwell on hallowed ground. From this sacred vantage point, cloaked against the harshness of decades past, I remember the good. I recall the sea edge that soothed my soul with its steady intrusion. I can still smell the forest glens that surrounded me and embraced me in their wooded reprieve. I find strength in the unfailing friendships that prayed me through uncertain travels. Deep inside I feel the forever warmth of Connie's steadfast love, the sureness of her dedication to our commitment to each other, and our shared devotion to our loving Father. I am eternally grateful to her for our journey together, one that is not only tender but also timeless and sure. I gather these treasures and place them before the Source of all the good and wondrous things of my life and stand back and gaze in wonder at their beauty.

I am at peace.

She is my life, and so I live.

His is the love I freely give.

God bless us all.

[T]HE LORD OF HOSTS WILL SPREAD A WON-drous feast for everyone around the world—a delicious feast of good food, with clear, well-aged wine and choice beef. At that time he will remove the cloud of gloom, the pall of death that hangs over the earth; he will swallow up death forever. The Lord God will wipe away all tears and take away forever all insults and mockery against his land and people. The Lord has spoken—he will surely do it! (Isaiah 25:6–8)

ACKNOWLEDGMENTS

AND IN THE END . . .

You have just read a love story, and as the 1967 recording by the Mamas and Papas goes, this book is "Dedicated to the One I Love," the one who is always there for me, my wife, my love, and my forever. God bless you, Connie.

Special thanks and deepest appreciation to my longtime friend, fellow rainbow-yawn mate, and diligent agent, Bucky Rosenbaum. Our journey together over the years has taken us to places that few have gone. We have remained encouraged and undaunted by the knowledge that no matter where God take us on this earth, one day we will end up in a place where everyone wants to be.

Gratitude and creative credit to Joel Miller for giving me the idea for this book. It became a reality because of his valuable contributions, imaginative input, and patient shaping of my ramblings into a recognizable tome. Also, thank you, Joel, for blessing me with talents of Jenn McNeil and Janene MacIvor—two of the best editors I have worked with.

Appreciation to David Schroeder, Betty Woodmancy, and Brian Mitchell, who have been a personal and integral part of my journey as an author. Peace and love, wherever you may be in our world of words by the time this book comes out.

Kindly kudos and Rumba reveries to Gabe Wicks who over the years has become my literary guide through the troubled waters of the publishing world. Thanks for administering the all-important final touch to our fourth book together.

Special acknowledgement to Marshall Terrill, who has read, edited, deleted, embraced, or been puzzled by almost every word I have written as an author. Thank you for your friendship and encouragement.

As with all my books, a tithe from the proceeds of *Stumbling on Open Ground* will go to Nancy Alcorn's incredible healing organization—Mercy Ministries. (mercyministries.org)

Most of all, praise God from whom all blessings flow.

God bless us all,

Ken Mansfield

NOTES

CHAPTER 4: CREDIT CARD STATEMENT

1. This figure is taken directly from cancer foundation's page under "Statistics."

CHAPTER 5: MISSING IN ATTITUDE
1. Matthew 16:17–19.
2. Matthew 16:23.

CHAPTER 6: "THE DOCK WILL SEE YOU NOW"
1. Psalm 46:10.

CHAPTER 11: ON THE ROAD AGAIN
1. Isaiah 45:9.

CHAPTER 14: TATTERED
1. "Shattered," Mick Jagger and Keith Richards, 1977.
2. "We Can Work It Out" Paul McCartney and John Lennon, 1965.

Chapter 16: Passing Understanding
1. "Trust and Obey," John H. Sammis and Daniel Towner, 1887.

Chapter 21: The Lightning at the End of the Tornado
1. Douglas Wilson, "The Potency of Right Worship," Credenda Agenda Website, December 4, 2009, http://www.credenda.org/index.php/Church/the-potency-of-right-worship.html.
2. Isaiah 61:3.

Chapter 24: Gideon
1. Judges 7.
2. Isaiah 42:10.
3. Psalm 46:10.

Chapter 25: If You Don't Know Me by Now
1. "If You Don't Know Me by Now," Kenny Gamble and Leon Huff, 1972.

Chapter 29: Heart of the Matter
1. James 5:16 AMP.

Chapter 31: Days of Yore—Daze of Your
1. Proverbs 26:11.

Chapter 32: Beauty and the Belief
1. Job 40:4–5.
2. Jan Dravecky, NIV Encouragement Bible, Zondervan.

ABOUT THE AUTHOR

Ken Mansfield, former US manager of the Beatles' Apple Record Company, Grammy/Dove award-winning producer and record-label executive during the exciting 60s, 70s, 80s, and 90s, now lives in the California Sierra Nevada mountains far from the madding crowds that filled his life for decades. When he and his wife Connie are not traveling between the mountains and ocean for inspiration, they spend most of their time on the road where Ken, an ordained minister and highly sought after public speaker, appears at churches, colleges, and events across the nation.

He is the author of three other books:
The Beatles, the Bible, and Bodega Bay
The White Book
Between Wyomings

Ken can be reached through these websites:
www.kmansfield.com
www.fabwhitebook.com
www.aubaycom.com

PRAISE FOR
KEN MANSFIELD'S MAGICAL
MINISTRY TOURS

Unique Outreach and Evangelism Events

"Ken's exciting outreach event gave us our biggest Saturday night attendance ever. We seat 2,200 and packed it out!"

—PASTOR LINCOLN BREWSTER, BAYSIDE COMMUNITY
CHURCH, SACRAMENTO CALIFORNIA

"Ken Mansfield inspired our people. The story of his transformed life spoke to the entire congregation. I know he will be a blessing to your church."

—DR. DAVID JEREMIAH, (TURNING POINT) SHADOW
MOUNTAIN CHURCH, EL CAJON, CALIFORNIA

"As featured speaker for the 2009 National Day of Prayer, at the Lake Charles LA Civic Center Coliseum, Ken mesmerized the audience and presented a dynamic way to reach out to lost people."

—BECKY MESTAYER, VP CHAIRPERSON, 2009 NATIONAL
DAY OF PRAYER, LAKE CHARLES, LOUISIANA

"God spoke to Parkside Church vicariously through the life of someone else. He sent in a prophet. The entire evening was a blessing."
—PASTOR ALISTAIR BEGGS (TRUTH FOR LIFE),
PARKSIDE CHURCH, CLEVELAND, OHIO

"Ken's appearance at our 2008 International Entertainment Buyers Association convention in Nashville was a 'highlight of the conference—it was amazing.'"
—TIFFANY DAVIS, EXECUTIVE DIRECTOR, INTEGRITY
EVENTS, INC., NASHVILLE, TENNESSEE

"Ken knocked it out of the park at Saddleback's Magnification Event. Everyone had a great time!"
—PASTOR RICK WARREN, SADDLEBACK CHURCH,
ORANGE COUNTY, CALIFORNIA

"As the guest speaker at our 2004 National Convention Ken offered a program that is both culturally enlightening and biblically relevant. He humbly communicated to everyone there."
—PHIL RYDMAN, DIRECTOR, ASSOCIATION OF GOSPEL
RESCUE MISSIONS, KANSAS CITY, MISSOURI

"Ken appeared at our midweek service—the attendance was spectacular and the ministry powerful. We were so excited that we brought him out to our Calvary Chapel Northwest Pastors Conference and, again, he was a huge hit with the six hundred pastors in attendance."
—PASTORS WAYNE TAYLOR AND BRETT WILLIAM, CALVARY
FELLOWSHIP, MT. LAKE TERRACE, WASHINGTON

"Ken Mansfield came to the State Prison at Jamestown, California, and gave his testimony at our Celebrate Recovery meeting. The men are still talking about it."
—GEORGE STEPHENS, PRISON MINISTRY
COORDINATOR, SCC STATE PRISON

Ken Mansfield's Magical Ministry Tours

"Ken Mansfield addressed our student body at two packed out chapel sessions. His testimony, stories about the music business and the Beatles were both fascinating and inspirational."

—Jeff Lockhart, Vice President for Development, Northwest University, Seattle, Washington

"I found myself almost speechless and the audience had the same reaction—they absolutely loved him. We received rave reviews in the weeks following his appearance."

—David Jenkins, Executive Director, Don Gibson Theatre, Shelby, North Carolina

"Ken has a moving life story from the Beatles to the Bible. His honest and compelling testimony is a must for communicating to the non-Christian world."

—Ian Leitch, Moody Bible Institute, Edinburgh, Scotland

For information on Ken's church, college, and special event appearances, go to: KMANSFIELD.COM

BETWEEN

 # WYOMINGS

My God and an iPod on the Open Road

A modern-day Ecclesiastes tale, *Between Wyomings* invites readers to travel with one of the most intriguing music executives of the twentieth century in a tender journey through the long and winding roads of the sixties and beyond. Along with his wife, Connie, and a van named Moses, Ken metaphorically recreates the drives that took him into the homes and careers of entertainment legends. As he considers the landscape of his soul for those exhilarating, lonely years, Ken calls readers to reflect on the highways of their own lives, the turns and deserts that press them into the heart of a Creator who has been there all along.

Somewhere between the smoky rooms

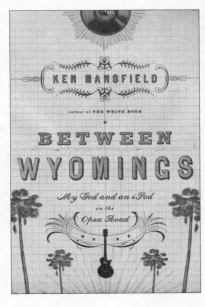

of a self-created life and the depths of a waiting ocean, Ken pulls out the worn Bible that smells of his aftershave and California mornings and remembers the grace that brought him to a new land. As Ken discovers, sometimes when we see how lost we are, we can finally begin to find home.

A cross between *Blue Highways* and *Blue Like Jazz*, *Between Wyomings* is iPod meets my God in the bound page, a road trip through the canyons of Hollywood, the outlaw alleys of Nashville, and the backstreets of the author's soul as this Grammy Award–winning producer recreates his journey through the lush landscape of success and the deserts that led him home.

PUBLISHED BY AU BAY COMMUNICATIONS
TO ORDER DIRECT FROM AUTHOR: WWW.AUBAYCOM.COM

the BEATLES
the BIBLE
and BODEGA BAY

MY LONG AND WINDING ROAD

Ken Mansfield can write authoritatively about the music business of the sixties and the Beatles because he was there in the midst of it—making it happen. As a young record label executive at Capitol Records, the Beatles were his clients, and they became his friends. Ken was hand-picked to be the first US manager of the Beatles' Apple Records and thrust into a world that would change his life forever. *The Beatles, the Bible and Bodega* Bay presents two portraits: the young man in London on top of the Apple building (and on top of the world!) as he watches the Beatles perform for the last time, and the older man on a remote Sonoma beach on his knees looking out to sea and into the heart of his Creator.

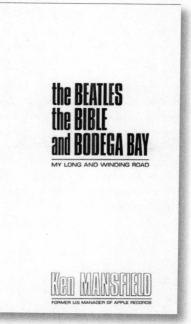

PUBLISHED BY AU BAY COMMUNICATIONS
TO ORDER DIRECT FROM AUTHOR: WWW.AUBAYCOM.COM

The WHITE BOOK

THE BEATLES, THE BANDS, THE BIZ: *An Insider's Look at an Era*

Ken Mansfield

THOMAS NELSON PUBLISHING

The WHITE BOOK

0300256

Through exclusive photographs and uniquely crafted personal stories, former US manager of Apple Records and Grammy Award–winning producer Ken Mansfield invites readers to know the characters of the Beatles and the musicians of their time—the bands that moved an industry and a culture to a whole new rhythm.

This engaging and unusual account spans some of the most fertile and intense decades in music history, including insight into celebrities such as Brian Wilson, Dolly Parton, Ray Orbison, Waylon Jennings, David Cassidy, and James Taylor. As the man who helped shape much of the music of the sixties and seventies, Ken Mansfield is in the rare position of observer, friend, and colleague of these sometimes quirky, sometimes ordinary, always talented individuals.

"Ken Mansfield and I shared the experience of the famous Apple rooftop session. There is no one better equipped to tell the Beatles' story—factually, from the inside."
ALAN PARSONS, ALAN PARSONS PROJECT, PRODUCER/ ENGINEER TO THE BEATLES/PINK FLOYD

"Ken was different, real California guy—the Beatles took to him straight away. He is one of the few insiders left that bore witness to the highs and lows of those insane days when we ruled the world."
JACK OLIVER, FORMER PRESIDENT OF APPLE RECORDS INTERNATIONAL

"I lived through the record industry's most exciting years with Ken. It is a pleasure to experience so much of it all again through the accuracy of his story telling and the clarity of his memory."
PETER ASHER, PETER & GORDON/A&R CHIEF APPLE RECORDS/MULTI PLATINUM PRODUCER

"Ken has a unique gift. I respect the affection he has for our game, and what he brought to it, will get you."
ANDREW LOOG OLDHAM, ROLLING STONES MANAGER AND PRODUCER

"In his 'White Book' Ken Mansfield salutes the Beatles as only a true insider can. Ken's book is the time machine that can travel back to that age of innocence that truly changed the world."
ROBIN LEACH, PRODUCER/HOST OF LIFESTYLES OF THE RICH & FAMOUS